The Tibetan Dhammapada

The Tibetan Dhammapada
Sayings of the Buddha

A translation of the Tibetan version of the
Udānavarga

Compiled by Dharmatrāta

Translated and introduced by
Gareth Sparham with guidance from
Lobsang Gyatso and Ngawang Thekchok

Edited by Beth Lee Simon

Wisdom Publications · London

First published in India in 1983
by Mahayana Publications, New Delhi

This revised edition published in 1986
Wisdom Publications
23 Dering Street, London W1, England

British Library Cataloguing in Publication Data
[Udānavarga. English] The Tibetan Dhammapada:
  sayings of the Buddha: a translation from the
  Tibetan of compilations of indicative verse
  (*Ched du brjod pa'i tshoms, Udānavarga*). —— Rev. ed.
  I. Dharmatrāta II. Sparham, Gareth III. Gyatso,
  Lobsang IV. Thekchok, Ngawang V. Simon, Beth Lee
  294.3'823   BQ1382.E5
ISBN 0 86171 012 6

Set in Plantin 11 on 13 point by
Setrite of Hong Kong, and printed
and bound by Eurasia Press of
Singapore and Biddles of Guildford,
Surrey, on 85gsm cream Graphic Text
paper supplied by Link Publishing
Papers of West Byfleet, Surrey.

Contents

Foreword
His Holiness the Dalai Lama

The practice of pacifying and improving the mind taught by Lord Buddha has been for over 2500 years one of the successful methods for achieving inner peace. It is an inestimable treasure of mankind. Today, many people are beginning to find in the Buddha's teaching an explanation of the human situation which accords with their own perception of reality. In consequence they are beginning to rely on his teaching to achieve the peace of mind they desire. As it becomes apparent to them that just external progress cannot bring lasting happiness, and that the hatred, greed and ignorance of their minds is standing between them and the happiness they seek, their respect for the relevance and profundity of Buddha's teaching grows.

The *Compilations of Indicative Verse (Udānavarga)*, newly translated here, is listed in the 108 volumes of Buddha's word translated into Tibetan, as *Ched du brjod pa'i tshoms*. It is known among Tibetans for the beauty of its poetry and the universality of its message. There is no Buddhist for whom the teaching of this book is irrelevant. Impermanence, the misery of cyclic existence, the harm of afflictive emotions, and the training and improvement of the mind with ethics, stabilization and intelligence are teachings common to all schools of Buddhism.

It is my hope that in the future all who wish to, may read the words of Buddha in their own language and find for themselves the peace and happiness they seek.

His Holiness the Fourteenth Dalai Lama
May 15, 1982

Preface to the Second Edition

Since the first edition of this translation of the Tibetan version of *Udānavarga* was published in New Delhi (by Mahayana Publications), I have become acquainted with an excellent Sanskrit critical edition of the text. Had I been able to consult it earlier there is no doubt the present translation would be even more faithful to the original than it is now.

However, there is definite benefit in reprinting the original translation, which was based entirely on Tibetan sources and traditional Tibetan scholarship. First, I hope it will hasten the appearance of a definitive edition of the *Udānavarga* that takes fully into account the various Tibetan sources. (It has become apparent in the last twenty years that serious Buddhist scholarship must, where possible, base itself primarily on Tibetan sources and use extant Sanskrit texts as an aid, not vice versa.) And second, I hope this book will help lay to rest, once and for all, the false notion of Tibetan Buddhism as somehow deficient in the older, authentic, teachings of the historical Buddha.

The translation in this new edition remains basically the same, with some changes in the Introduction and the spelling of religious titles systematized.

I would like to acknowledge the help of Dr. N. Ribush whose continued enthusiasm for this book has been a major factor in its appearance.

Gareth Sparham
Vancouver, BC
March 1985

Introduction

Homage to the Buddha, Doctrine and Community.

In the spring of 1975, while studying Maitreya's interpretation of the *Perfection of Wisdom* (*Prajñāpāramitā, Shes rab kyi pha rol tu phyin pa*), Lobsang Gyatso, my teacher and the principal of the Buddhist Dialectic School in Dharamsala, in the north of India, called me into his study to discuss a project. He said that while re-reading the *Compilations of Indicative Verse* (*Udānavarga, Ched du brjod pa'i tshoms*) he had been struck by its relevance and he felt it important that Western people just beginning their study of Mahāyāna Buddhism should have access to such material. He then explained six of the compilations to me, and later that year we published them in a small booklet.

Over the next few years, while studying the texts of Asaṅga, Nāgārjuna, Chandrakīrti, and Maitreya, we continued to work slowly through the remaining compilations. The relation between the viewpoint presented in this sūtra and that of Asaṅga and other later Indian Mahāyāna writers slowly began to come into focus.

After I had made a rough translation of the entire text based

on the explanations of Lobsang Gyatso, I spent the next two
winters with Ngawang Tekchok at Sera Monastery in
Karnataka, south India, going through the text from
beginning to end. In the mornings, we worked on the
translation, and in the afternoons I studied Dharmakīrti's
Commentary to (Dignāga's) 'Compendium of Valid Cognition'
(*Pramāṇavārtika, Tshad ma rnam 'grel*). In the evenings, the
peace of the monastery would again turn my thoughts to a
comparison between the Mahāyāna Buddhism of the debate
tradition and that of the Hīnayāna presented in the
Compilations. I could see the strong and necessary relationship
between them.

I had nearly finished rechecking our entire translation of the
Compilations against the long *Commentary to 'Compilations of
Indicative Verse'* (*Udānavarga-vivaraṇa, Ched du brjod pa'i
tshoms kyi rnam par 'grel pa*) by Prajñāvarman when I learned
of an earlier translation of the same text by W. Woodville
Rockhill.[1]

It seemed to me that while Rockhill had produced a useful
piece of work, my new translation of the *Compilations* would
be an improvement upon the very valuable one that Rockhill
had done. In particular, the extensive training in the scholastic
tradition of Buddhism that I had received made me more
familiar with both the technical language of the text and the
specifics of the mental development being presented. Therefore I have been able to avoid some of the difficulties Rockhill
faced in this regard. Also, I have made use of my close
association with some of the learned Tibetan Buddhists who
have settled as refugees in India to decipher the more obscure
parts of Prajñāvarman's *Commentary*, and to make sense of
passages Rockhill was unable to understand. Finally, I think I
have paid the necessary attention to verse and language that
this text in particular deserves.

When I was talking with Ling Rinpoche, who was head of
the Ge-lug (*dGe lugs*) school of Tibetan Buddhists and senior
tutor to the Dalai Lama, I told him that I had translated
this work. He asked immediately if I had kept it in verse.
There is a beauty and life in the poetic language of the

Compilations that is an integral part of the whole. To ignore this, as Rockhill did to a great extent, is to lose a vital part of the original.

In early 1982 I completed the final version, which I felt to be highly readable and accurate. By this time, I had spent many years thinking about the ideas in the book. Because its teachings on renunciation, on the value of the life of the monk and nun, and on simplicity and calmness were basic to the complete teaching of Buddha that Tibetan Buddhism offers, I decided to make the book available to as many interested people as possible.

The *Compilations* might present a problem to those Buddhists like myself who are attracted to the Mahāyāna concept of *bodhicitta* — the altruistic wish to be a Buddha to benefit other beings. The teaching seems to be directed to persons set on obtaining personal release from the miseries of cyclic existence and not to the Mahāyāna practitioner. It extols the state of the Foe Destroyer (*arhan, dgra bcom pa*) and does not exhort the reader to forsake personal liberation for the sake of others. It could be thought that the teaching is less noble and the practices not relevant to a person who values altruism most highly. That such a view is wrong is attested to by Atīśa, the eleventh century Bengali writer, who was instrumental in the re-emergence, clarification and second spreading of Buddhism in Tibet. In his *Lamp for the Path to Enlightenment* (*Bodhi-pathapradīpa, bYang chub lam gyi sgron ma*) he writes that every teaching of Buddha is to be considered as personal advice to be applied to one's own practice. To think that a certain teaching is for somebody else is a mistake.

How then is the new practitioner with an interest in the Mahāyāna, or particularly in the Mantrayāna, to approach this type of teaching? How should such a person integrate the teaching of the *Compilations* into an overall Mahāyāna practice?

In general, in Tibetan Buddhist literature, one finds the *Compilations* quoted in two contexts: validating an explanation of a practice, or substantiating a tenet. In Tsong

14 The Tibetan Dhammapada

Khapa's *Great Exposition of the Graded Path* (*Lam rim chen mo*) for example, the *Compilations* is quoted to summarize explanations of how to meditate on karma, death, misery, and so on. In his *Commentary on the Difficult Points* [*in the Mind Only Presentation*] *of Basis of All* (*Kun gzhi dKa' 'grel*) the *Compilations* is quoted by those arguing for only one consciousness.

More specifically we find the *Compilations* used in relation to two types of practices in Tibetan Mahāyāna Buddhism. Firstly, for guidance in ethics which calm the mind. The Kadam-pa (*bKa' gdams pa*) tradition of Tibetan Buddhism, which originated with Atiśa and flourished until the time of Tsong Khapa, accorded the book a special place as one of their six treasures. It is said that the great Ka-dam-pa lamas took the *Jātaka Tales* (*Jātaka-mālā, sKyes pa rabs kyi rgyud*) and the *Compilations* as their main source for proper ethics and conduct (the first of the three higher trainings).

Secondly, the gate that separates Mahāyāna from all other Buddhist teachings is *bodhicitta,* the altruistic motivation to become a Buddha for the sake of others. Mahāyāna teachings stress again and again that where this wish is present in the mindstream the person's practice becomes a Mahāyāna practice, and where it is absent even meditation on emptiness or on tantric deities cannot be classified as Mahāyāna meditation. Therefore, for those sincerely interested in the Mahāyāna practices, no meditations are more important than those that develop *bodhicitta* and compassion, the mind-state that precedes actual *bodhicitta*. Indeed, as Chandrakīrti stresses in the opening lines of his *Supplement to the Middle Way* (*Madhyamakāvatāra, dBu ma la 'jug pa*) meditation on compassion and *bodhicitta* is important not only at the beginning of the Mahāyāna practice — it is always the most important practice. Chandrakīrti uses three similes: at the beginning of practice, compassion is like a seed, during the long and arduous travel along the Mahāyāna path it is like water given to the seed, and at the time of the achievement of the results of Buddha, compassion is like the ripening of the crops.

Dignāga, one of the architects of the basic Mahāyāna structure of logic and inference, holds compassion to be the starting point, or the basis from which it is valid to infer that Buddhas do exist. His *Compendium of Valid Cognition* (*Pramāṇasamuccaya, Tshad ma kun btus*) opens with these words:

> Homage to the One who became a Valid Cognizer,
> The Helper of Migrators, Teacher, Tathāgata and
>   Refuge.

The first line refers to the result, the omniscient state of buddhahood, and the four epithets in the second line to the mental development of a person who is moving towards buddhahood. In Dignāga's view, compassion directed towards all that lives (the 'Helper of the Migrators'), is first and foremost.

In Mahāyāna literature there are two main explanations about meditating on compassion and *bodhicitta*. The one that comes from Maitreya through Asaṅga is known as the 'sevenfold method' and the other, which comes from Śāntideva, is known as 'exchanging self with others.' The meditations in both methods are based on achieving equanimity, a prerequisite for further development. This equanimity, and the meditational practices by which it is attained are common to all schools of Indo-Tibetan Buddhist practice. The four immeasurables cited in the *Compilations,* equanimity, great love, great compassion and great bliss, are based on it.

The meditations in both methods generate a strong feeling of empathy for the misery and causes of misery experienced by all sentient beings. In the former method one thinks about all beings as if they were one's mother. With the latter, one investigates the mistaken view of one's own existence, and contemplates the faults of selfishness and the good results of cherishing others. In both lineages equanimity, great love and great compassion are the high goals. By thinking about the mode of cyclic existence we see our true relationship with all other beings, and by remembering their past kindnesses, we

generate love for them. Then, by bringing to mind their
hardships, we generate compassion and the wish to help them.
These practices are prerequisites for attaining success in all
further Mahāyāna practices.

The main practice taught in the *Compilations* is the understanding of the four noble truths vis-à-vis the practitioner. By
contemplating the twelve links of dependent arising, the practitioner understands impermanence and selflessness, the afflictive emotions, and the reality of personal misery and its cause;
in consequence, the wish to be freed from this pervading state
of suffering arises. After contemplating the first two truths in
this way, the attainment of personal freedom or nirvana (the
true cessation) becomes one's aim. The method to achieve it is
what has been called by some the Hīnayāna path.

The more thoroughly such meditations are practised, the
greater the understanding of the suffering of existence and its
causes arise. An ever-stronger wish to be freed from cyclic
existence grows in proportion to that understanding. Recog-
nizing the similarities between one's own situation and that of
others, a wish for all beings to be free becomes as strong or
even stronger than that of desiring one's own personal
liberation. As Tsong Khapa says in his *Great Exposition of the
Graded Path*,

> Thinking about this [the four truths] in relation to
> others, the cause that gives rise to *bodhicitta* comes
> about.

Jamyang Shepa (*'jam-dhyangs bzhad-pa*), writing in the late
sixteenth century, says in his commentary to the second
chapter of Dharmakīrti's *Commentary to* (Dignāga's)'*Compendium of Valid Cognition*' that the Hīnayāna Foe Destroyer
practises mental development up to the fifth stage, and
develops great compassion. To back up his contention that
such a strong compassion is generated on the Hīnayāna path,
he refers to Tsong Khapa's *Great Exposition of the Graded
Path* in which a passage from the *Sūtra of the Question of
Sāgara-mati (Ārya-Sāgaramati-pariprcchā-mahāyāna-sūtra,
'phags pa blo gros rgya mtshos zhus pa zhes bya ba theg pa chen*

po'i mdo) is explained. The passage is as follows:

> Sāgara-mati, there was a trader or a land-owner who had an only son. He looked on his son with attachment, affection and closeness, and saw him as beautiful. He could see nothing wrong in him at all. This boy, when he grew older, fell into a cesspool while he was playing. The mother and other relatives, seeing their boy fallen into the pool, raised up a great commotion and set to wailing in distress. However, they did not go into the dirty pool to get him out. Then the father of the boy came to that place and saw that his son had fallen into the cesspool. When he saw him, in a complete rush, with his mind overcome with the wish to extricate his son, he plunged into the cesspool without any feeling of revulsion, and pulled the boy out.

The cesspool is the three realms, and the boy is all sentient beings. The mother and relatives who wail in distress but are without the ability to extricate (the child) are the Hearers and Solitary Realizers. The father is the Bodhisattva. The sūtra says that Hearers and Solitary Realizers have a compassion like that of the mother for a dear child who has fallen into a dirty pool. The love and compassion of both the mother and father in the story are equal in breadth. Anyone with such a mind could not be considered 'selfish.' To highlight the great commitment of the Bodhisattva, or as a means to motivate the suitable person into going yet a step further and promising to undertake the task of freeing every living creature from misery, a word like 'selfish' is occasionally used to compare a Bodhisattva to other types of practitioners. As the quotation above makes clear, the difference between the mother's mind and the father's is the personal commitment or vow to benefit others by becoming a Buddha, turning the wheel of the Dharma and leading all to liberation.

The teaching of the *Compilations* should be taken as personal advice by those who wish to follow the Mahāyāna path. By following this advice we can recognize clearly our own suffering; consequently we can go that step further and generate a strong empathy for the same suffering that all other beings must bear.

The Buddha, who is credited with saying the verses gathered in this book, lived about 2,500 years ago in the north of India. He is said to have been born in Lumbini, now just a poor Nepalese village about ten miles from the Indian border, and to have spent most of his life travelling and teaching in the part of the Gangetic Plain now called Bihar and Uttar Pradesh. Even today the traveller in these parts of India and Nepal can see the remains of huge temples and monasteries bearing witness to his birth, life and *parinirvāṇa*. This historical Buddha was called Siddhārtha in the earlier part of his life and Śākyamuni or Gautama Buddha after he attained enlightenment at Bodh Gaya. Moved by the force of his compassion for all living beings, Śākyamuni Buddha taught extensively in accord with the temperaments and aptitudes of his disciples.

Later, after he passed into nirvana, his disciples met together to recite the teachings of the Buddha that each had memorized. The reciter of the moment would sit on a throne made up of all the mats of the assembled monks. It is said that all of those present at the convocations were Foe Destroyers, each of whom had achieved the last body. These memorized teachings of Buddha were then handed down orally from generation to generation until they were put into written form (at a later date).

The structuring of the *Compilations* is primarily determined, then, by a pattern of oral transmission within a religious context. The *Compilations* are not a single or even ongoing discourse of the Buddha faithfully recorded by a scribe. Nor does it consist of the words of the Buddha in the order in which they were recited by the Foe Destroyers at that first covocation after the Buddha's *parinirvāṇa*. It is, rather, a compilation of verses taken from the words of Buddha and arranged later into a string of thirty-three topics, following a loose but not entirely arbitrary order. This method of compilation explains similarities between this book and the *Dhammapada* of the Pali canon. Although, as Rockhill has shown, all the verses of the *Dhammapada* are included in the *Compilations* (though sometimes with slight variations) their order is different. Also the *Dhammapada* does not include some of the verses found here. Nevertheless, despite differences, both books are included in the corpus of Buddha's teaching.

Rockhill, who translated this collection at the end of the nineteenth century, says that the verses *(udāna)* are probably concluding stanzas uttered by Buddha to summarize discourse. This would appear to be true of many of the verses which use a series of epithets to describe stages in the path or qualities of mind. Some of the verses, however, contain references to specific events and it is more likely that these were uttered aphoristically when the opportunity to exemplify a precept or idea presented itself. In any case, the words *ched du brjod pa* in the Tibetan title can mean an utterance directed to some specific person, or an utterance to indicate or highlight some important meaning.

Prajñāvarman interprets the title with the second signification and points to the opening verse, 'Alas: composites are impermanent....' as indicating the teaching of the four truths. Nevertheless, the first signification is possible also because many of the verses are directed towards specific individuals.

The compiler of these verses was a Foe Destroyer called Dharmatrāta (*Chos skyob*) who lived somewhere between 75 B.C. and 200 A.D. Since the Tibetan version says only that the verses were translated from an Indian language, it is not known whether the original was in Sanskrit, Pāli or a vernacular Prakrit language. The text was translated into Tibetan by Vidyāprabhākara. Although the date of the translation is not firmly established, the likelihood is that it was done in the ninth century.[2]

This brings us to two popular misconceptions about Tibetan Buddhism. The first is that Tibetan Buddhism is a

Buddhism that excludes nirvana as a worthy goal. The second is that what became the dominant religion of Tibet is not Buddhism at all but some type of degenerate Lamaism or Shamanism. Neither of these stances is correct. A new presentation of this book translated from the Tibetan and explained to me by two Tibetan monks (Ngawang Tekchok, the former abbot of Sera-mey Monastery, and Lobsang Gyatso, the principal of the Buddhist School in Dharmsala,) will do much to dispel these two wrong ideas. The Buddhist tradition, which stresses discipline, the simple life and the attainment of liberation in a forest retreat, is very much alive amongst Tibetans.

The basic text for this translation of *Compilations* is catalogued under *La* in the *mdo mang* section of the *sNar thang* edition of the *bKa' 'gyur* (in the personal library of the Fourteenth Dalai Lama). This was compared with the *sDe dge* edition of the *bKa' 'gyur* published by the late Karmapa Rinpoche and donated by him to the Buddhist School of Dialectics. Most of the differences between the two editions are in spelling mistakes. Where differences in meaning do occur, the interpretation of Prajñāvarman is followed wherever possible. Where alternative readings are possible, the alternative has been given in a footnote.

The Three Realms

Western cosmology provides us with a blueprint for organizing an expanding, external universe. That our minds can grapple with and order the interlocking complexities presented by modern mathematics and physics is testimony to our ability to accustom ourselves to a variety of heterogeneous concepts.

In the same way, we can grasp the picture of existence presented in Buddhism. Buddhist cosmology deals primarily with a universe based on one's own mind. In the view of Buddhist masters, familiarity with the Buddhist 'blueprint' holds more than intellectual interest for the practitioner because from familiarity comes the understanding of it, and from understanding one develops a well-founded faith; thorough understanding combined with solid faith are then used as the basis for freedom from cyclic existence.

Buddhist cosmology posits a three-tiered, self-enclosed universe. The universe is self-enclosed in the sense that all phenomena are contained within it, and any activity produced by self-grasping results in rebirth somewhere within it. Therefore all beings except Buddhas and completed Foe Destroyers exist somewhere within the realms.

The first or lowest realm is the realm of desire. The human level is one of the six divisions of the desire realm, the others being the hell, hungry ghosts, animals, anti-gods and gods. The middle realm is the realm of form. It has four divisions characterized by four concentrations. (*dhyāna, bsam gtan*). (See note 67.) In the formless realm, as indicated by its name, beings lack the aggregate of form. This realm also has four divisions. Beings in this realm pass extremely long lives absorbed in such thoughts as the infinity of space or of consciousness, eventually eliminating all objects of thought. But this realm too, like the realms of desire and form, is part of the cycle of existence. The basic activities of the form and formless realms are the practices of increasing absorption into ever more subtle mental states. Both Buddhists and non-Buddhists can achieve the attainments of the upper realms.

The Four Truths and Twelve Links

When Buddha, having achieved enlightenment at Bodh Gaya, first taught at Sarnath, he said to his five disciples,

> This is, for the Superior, true misery.

The principal true misery he had in mind at that time was the aggegrates of form and consciousness associated with beings migrating endlessly through the universe just described. Just as the aggregate of form is included in the physical universe, similarly none of the aggregates is thought of as being separate from the three realms. The aggregates of a being in the realm of desire are included in the realm of desire itself, (with the exception of certain aspects of a developed consciousness like calm abiding, etc.) Every creature in the realms of desire and form is circumscribed by the five aggregates of form, feeling, discrimination, consciousness and variable phenomena. In the formless realm there is no aggregate of form. The concept of aggegrates or accumulations of physical or conscious elements associated with living beings is used to differentiate certain groups of constituents from the broad spectrum of the total constituents of the universe.

Having taught true misery the Buddha then referred to afflictive emotions (*kleśa, nyon mongs*) and actions (*karma, las*) with the words,

These are, for the Superior, the true origin.

The Buddha didn't teach in terms of consciousness and sub-consciousness as we typically understand these terms. He taught that the root of all afflictive emotion, which motivates unskilful actions, is an innate view of a self-sufficient, substantially existing person. It grasps at a truly existing person and gives rise to strong emotional states of longing or antagonism. These afflict the mind and motivate actions that create in turn the potential (i.e. karma) for future aggregates, for again taking birth within cyclic existence.

The remaining two truths, the truth of cessation and the truth of the path (by which cessation is achieved), were taught by the Buddha in the same famous sermon at Sarnath. Cessation, which in its completed stage is called nirvana, is dealt with extensively in the compilation of verses called 'Seeing' (page 134). Cessation seems to be fundamental in nature. It can be compared to preventing the throwing of a stone into a still clear pond of water; the cessation of the ripples is nothing but the clear still pond itself. The true path includes the uncontaminated paths of seeing, meditation and no more learning. They are discussed below.

The twelve interdependent links are mentioned often

throughout the *Compilations of Indicative Verse*. They are dealt with at length in the compilation of verses called 'Nirvana' (page 129) which is a wider explanation of the four truths and a description of how a person comes to enter cyclic existence and how liberation from cyclic existence can occur. The twelve component links are: ignorance, composites (i.e. action), consciousness, name and form, (i.e. the five aggregrates), the six sources, contact, feeling, craving, attachment, becoming, birth, old age and death.

Each earlier component or link provides the basis for the arising of the subsequent ones. Thus ignorance or unknowing (the wrong view of self referred to above) is normally the motivation for actions and is therefore the basis for them. The progressive unfolding of the links describes the entry to cyclic existence. Their elimination describes liberation.

It is said that Buddha taught the twelve links of interdependent arising as the antidote to ignorance. It is considered by many practitioners to be one of the most difficult ideas in Buddhist meditations. In essence, though, it means that all phenomena arise in dependence. For example, dying is intimately related with birth and dependent upon it. It is said that as one's understanding of dependent arising in general develops, the understanding of how these link relate becomes clearer and more profound.

The Path and Thirty-seven Factors of Enlightenment

The path to freedom from all forms of existence within any of the three realms is not an external one, but rather a development and refinement of mind. The path has five stages. The first, called the path of accumulation, is the longest and most varied of the five. A person's mind enters this stage at the moment the idea of renunciation arises. (Renunciation is the conscious decision to achieve liberation from the misery of the three realms.) This stage lasts until the achievement of a meditational practice that is the same in content as the actual meditation that frees a person from cyclic existence. With the

achievement of such a meditation one enters the path of preparation. There are four stages to this path as the mind gets
closer to the direct non-conceptual realization of the four
truths and the actual mode of existence. When that realization
finally dawns, the mind, now on the path of seeing, and its
object selflessness, become non-dual, like pouring water into
water. It is said that mind on the path of seeing experiences
two moments: in the first, intellectual misconceptions and
doubts about such things as the four truths are eliminated; in
the second moment it realizes freedom from those. On the
path of meditation, or cultivation, one develops and deepens
the direct non-conceptual realization made on the path of
seeing, and all the innate, basic defilements are eliminated.
These defilements are said to be big, middling, and small, and
the states of mind that eliminate them are said to be the small,
middling and big paths of meditation respectively. The
defilements are likened to stains in a cloth, and the path of
meditation to scrubbing the cloth clean. The last instant of the
path of meditation is called the vajralike stabilization. After
this instant, nirvana is attained. With the attainment of
nirvana, the mind is called the path of no more learning.

This explanation of the way to achieve liberation via
five stages is a metaphor. The direct explanation is in
terms of the thirty-seven factors of enlightenment. These
thirty-seven factors are the four mindfulnesses, the four
complete abandonments, the four legs of miracles, the five
powers, the five strengths, the seven branches of enlightenment and the noble eightfold path. They are reducible to
ten basic mental factors: faith, perseverance, remembrance,
intelligence, stabilization, equanimity, joy, conceptualization,
ethics and pliancy. At different stages of the path, different
factors are said to play greater or lesser roles. According to one
explanation, remembrance (or mindfulness), perseverance and
stabilization are important at the earlier, intermediate and
later stages of the path of accumulation respectively. The
remembrance of the four truths gives understanding of what is
to be done and what is to be abandoned. Then one needs

perseverance at the task; this yields stability of mind. Faith, enthusiastic perseverance, remembrance, intelligence and stabilization are the primary mental factors on the path of preparation. Without faith, the mind would not be motivated to contemplate the four truths. Perseverance overcomes laziness which prevents the work. Stabilization prevents the mind from wandering, while remembrance of the truths presents the object for analysis.

At the time of non-conceptual understanding, i.e. the path of seeing, remembrance keeps the mind from forgetting the subject; perseverance overcomes laziness, and physical and mental joy are experienced as the benefits of this stage. Pliancy and stability of mind are mental factors which provide the foundation and continuing situation for the absence of afflictive emotions, while equanimity is the mental factor which precludes afflictive emotions by its very nature. In the final stages of practice the factors which deliver the person into nirvana are the perfect view (intelligence which understands what was realised in meditation), perfect remembrance, perfect perseverance, perfect stabilization, perfect conceptualization (which serves as the preceding impetus to realization), perfect limitation of action, perfect speech and perfect livelihood. These last three are included in ethics which is a mental factor guarding the person from doing wrong.

The Eight Superior Beings

There are eight types of Superior Being. These eight are the four 'Enterers' to a particular fruit or result of practice, and the four 'Abiders' in these fruits or results. 'Superior' is a designation limited to those who have achieved the path of seeing. They are the Enterer and Abider in the Result of Stream Enterer, Enterer and Abider in the Result of Once-returner, Enterer and Abider in the Result of Non-returner, and Enterer and Abider in the Result of Foe-Destroyer. Usually the four beings who are abiding in the result or fruit of their work are referred to by the abbreviated names, Stream Enterer, Once-returner, Non-returner and Foe Destroyer.

The Four Immeasurables

The practitioner who wants to achieve nirvana cultivates immeasurable love, immeasurable compassion, immeasurable joy and immeasurable equanimity. Through the force of meditation on these the practitioner avoids doing any harm to others and teaches others the method to benefit themselves. As well as the results, the meditations themselves are called 'immeasurable' because the object of observation of each meditation includes all sentient beings who are as immeasurable as space. Love, here, is the desire or wish that all beings be happy. Compassion is the desire or wish that they all be free of misery. Joy and intense pleasure arise at their happiness and freedom from misery. Equanimity and tolerance is evenness of mind towards all beings; unpleasantness and kindness do not cause dislike or emotionally afflictive liking, respectively to arise and disturb it.

The Result

The result is called nirvana. Nirvana means passing beyond misery. One who attains nirvana is called a Foe Destroyer, because the Foe Destroyer has eliminated or destroyed the real foe — afflictive emotions — for ever. There are two stages to nirvana called nirvana with remainder and nirvana without remainder. Nirvana with remainder is attained by the Foe Destroyer who still has contaminated aggregates. Such a Foe Destroyer has, however, eliminated every cause to take any future rebirth. At death, therefore, the aggregates fall away and the final stage, nirvana without the remainder of the aggregates, is achieved.

Poem

Beyond the levels of the three-tiered universe
There is an island rising from a storm-tossed sea.
Seen from the ship at daybreak, rising far across the waves.
It seems to weary hearts the journey's final end.
For travellers it is a place where wind will not
Drive cold and salty water on a freezing deck,
Where boards that creak even at night
No longer rise incessantly to meet the tired.
There the movement of the boat will cease.
The wind that blows will only serve to cool.
Now closer, the gardens of the island seem
Clear in the golden sunshine of the noonday sky.
The fatigue of the journey is now left behind,
Each sailor works with others in the task
To quickly sail the ocean in between
The boat and freedom from unending work.
Who knows for sure if there's an island there?
Let others argue. Working if need be until the sea
Itself goes dry, let's set the ship for shore.
We'll be happy if we get there
And anyway, we'll make a better crew.

G.S.

Order of Compilations

1 *Impermanence*

The compilation of verses about impermanence is first because the mistaken idea of permanence is the basis for the arising of all afflictive emotions. From those afflictive emotions arise non-virtuous actions and from those actions come misery. Therefore we can block afflictive emotions by understanding impermanence. When afflictive emotions do not arise, we have no cause to create non-virtue. Then happiness is achieved.

2 *Desire*

Understanding impermanence leads to renunciation. The object of renunciation is the end of desire. Therefore the verses about desire are second.

3 *Craving*

The verses on craving serve two purposes. The primary religious aim is to promote and encourage the practitioner to remove great longing for objects of desire. Secondly, and historically, these verses also stand in opposition to the Jain belief that removal of objects that seem to produce happiness eliminates desire.

4 *Caution*

Caution follows next because the antidote to craving is caution. Prajñāvarman's *Commentary* says caution is that which fully protects mind from contamination and the grounds of contamination.

5 *Beauty*

The compilation of verses about beauty follows that of caution because even those who value caution can be distracted by beauty and waste their lives.

6 *Ethics*

The compilation of verses about ethics follows beauty because when one ceases to view objects as possessing beauty or ugliness (i.e. as friend or enemy), then one's ethics become perfect.

7 *Fine Conduct*

Fine conduct here should be understood as the essence of ethical behaviour. 'Fine' connotes pure and clear.

8 *Words*

The compilation of verses about words makes the point that ethics and fine conduct are concerned with more than physical behaviour. Ethical behaviour includes good verbal conduct.

9 *Actions*

The compilation of verses about bad actions teaches the importance of eliminating all unskilful or non-virtuous action.

10   *Faith*

The compilation of verses about faith follows actions because it is the means by which such bad actions are eliminated. 'Faith' means a complete openness of mind. There are two aspects of faith: complete trust and yearning. The former is said to precede the latter.

11   *The Ordained Person*

Using faith as a basis, the practitioner generates the path of a Superior. We can surmise that this compilation of verses was addressed to an audience made up for the most part of people who had taken one of the sets of ordination vows, either the novice vows for males or females or the full ordination vows for males or females.

12   *The Path*

Two types of religious persons are described in the preceding set of verses: the conventional and the ultimate. The ultimate religious person is a Foe Destroyer without any contaminated aggregates. By following 'the superior path' a person achieves such a state. Therefore the set of verses concerning 'the path' follows that of ordained persons. (See also Introduction p. 15 et al.)

13   *Honours*

Honours, the trappings and esteem of others, hinders the cultivation of the path taught in the preceding section; therefore the verses concerning honours are given next. Honours include not only gifts of money and food, but also respect, homage and the ministrations of admirers.

14   *Animosity*

Since animosity toward more wealthy religious practitioners comes from one's desire to receive presents and the service of others, this compilation of verses about animosity follows that concerning honours.

15 *Mindfulness*

The method to remove animosity is the cultivation of mindfulness. Therefore the compilation of verses about mindfulness follows animosity.

16 *Miscellaneous*

The compilation of miscellaneous or various collected verses follows mindfulness. It includes explanations of what causes mindfulness to decline and the antidotes to such decline. The title of this section literally means 'little bits,' or 'separate little works.'

17 *Water*

Since enthusiasm and mindfulness, like water, settle the dust of scattered mind taught in the above miscellaneous verses, the compilation of verses about water comes next.

18 *The Flower*

The preceding verses about water are presented as a dialectic—posing 'good' water against 'bad'; this present compilation about flowers is constructed in the same way. Just as nectar and beauty are produced by the flower, the path to liberation blossoms in the mind of the practitioner. The other side of the coin is that the pretty but passing nature of a flower is like the nature of cyclic existence. The conclusion is that just as the eyes turn away from the flower when its beauty has faded, the mind should renounce the transiency of this world.

19 *The Horse*

At the end of the compilation of verses about flowers we find the example of the flower in the pond being plucked out by its root. This exemplified the elimination of such afflictions as

hatred, etc. The contaminated flowers of desire, craving, hate
and so on are plucked from the good mind. The good mind,
having such qualities as faith and stability, is like a good horse,
so the compilation of verses comparing the good mind to a
horse is next.

20   Wrath

Wrath is the vicious state of mind that precedes a malicious
deed. When the mind is subdued, wrath is eliminated. Therefore, the compilation of verses about wrath follows that on
taming the horse, i.e. the mind.

21   The One Gone Thus

The One Gone Thus (tathāgata, de bzhin gshegs pa) has gone
along the path of earlier Buddhas. He has given up wrath,
practised the six perfections and through compassion achieved
the state of a Buddha. Therefore the compilation of verses
about the One Gone Thus is next.

22   Listening

Since an important method by which the Ones Gone Thus
benefit others is through explaining the doctrine, the next
compilation of verses on listening is an exhortation to listen to
what they have to say. Unless one listens to them, the
Buddhas cannot help. Listening means to focus the thinking-
mind by directing the hearing sense-consciousness towards
sounds.

23   Self

Since the result of listening is the pacification of self, this
compilation of verses about self follows.

24   Comparisons

Only those who have tamed their mind, those who are their

own masters, can realize the truth in the comparisons. Therefore the compilation of verses containing comparisons is next.

25 Intimate Friends

After having listened to the teaching and decided to make an effort to practise, one should then give up bad companions and rely on the dearest friends, one's spiritual teachers.

26 Nirvana

By giving up wrong-doing and relying on spiritual friends, nirvana is achieved. The compilation of verses about nirvana therefore comes next.

27 Seeing

Only with pure view can the nirvana just taught be achieved. In order to teach this the compilation of verses about seeing or realizing the view is next.

28 Evil

With perfect view virtue is embraced and evil cast away. Therefore, the compilation of verses about evil follows. The earlier compilation of verses about fine conduct gave the positive side of action motivated by perfect view. This compilation explains what is to be given up.

29 Antitheses

In general, this compilation of verses points to the difference between the good and bad explained in the earlier compilations on fine conduct and evil. It explains that those who have abandoned all evil and done all virtue outshine everyone.

30   *Happiness*

This compilation of verses concerns the happiness that results from embracing fine conduct and rejecting evil.

31   *The Mind*

Since happiness is based on the mind itself, the compilation of verses about mind follows that on happiness. A monk who wanted to leave his retreat came to tell Buddha of his wish. Buddha said, 'Do not go where your mind wants to take you; calm your mind, for peace and happiness are brought by a mind that is calm.'

32   *The Monk*

The ultimate monk or nun is someone who has a subdued mind. Such a person has both physical and mental detachment: the former means having no home, and the latter, no longing desire.

33   *The Brahmin*

A Brahmin is a person who is completely clean and pure, cleansed of all inner and outer defilement. Therefore, the concluding compilation of verses is about Brahmins.

Folio One

Homage to the omniscient one
May all good fortune come about

1 *Impermanence*

1 I will relate correctly[3] here
   The Conqueror's indicative teachings.
   Dispel dullness and sleepiness
   And listen well with a joyful mind.

2 The Protector, the All-knowing One,
   The Mighty, the All-merciful,
   The Holder of the last body,
   The Bhagavan[4] spoke out these words.[5]

3 Alas! composites are impermanent,
   They start to perish when they are produced.
   Since having arisen they perish;
   Calming them down is happiness.

4 How can any person know joy
   Or pleasure in such a hot blaze?[6]
   Why don't those living in the dark
   Make an effort to find a torch?

5 What joy is there in this [body], seeing
   These pigeon-coloured discarded bones
   Just lying scattered here and there
   Where they were tossed upon the ground?

6   From that same moment of the night
    Humans first enter in the womb
    The journey of their life to death begins.
    Once gone there is no turning back.

7   At daybreak many people can be seen,
    That evening one is gone from sight;
    At evening many people can be seen,
    Next morning one is gone from sight.

8   Since many girls and boys have died
    While young and in the prime of life,
    How can one feel secure and think,
    'I'm young so I have long to live'?

9   Some die when they are in the womb,
    Some on the ground where they are born,
    Some die just as they learn to crawl
    And some just as they learn to walk.

10 Some die old, and some die young,
    Some in the very prime of life.
    All people pass away in turn
    Just like the fall of ripened fruit.

11 As all ripe fruit
    Always falls and rots,
    So all who are born
    Are always by their deaths destroyed.

12 Like every pot
    A skilful potter moulds from clay,
    Which finally is broken and destroyed,
    So too is every person's life.

13 Like weaving wool
    Stretched back and forth across a loom
    Finally runs out,
    So too is every person's life.

14 Like every step of one condemned
   Brings nearer the gallows
   Where that one will hang and die,
   So too is every person's life.

15 Just as a waterfall's flow
   Can never turn back on itself,
   So a person's life goes on forever
   Without increase, without return.

16 So hard [to obtain] and yet so short[7]
   And yet with so much misery,
   Lives are obliterated so soon,
   Like words written with a stick in water.

17 Just like the herder with a stick
   Who drives the flocks into the fold,
   So age and sickness drive all humans
   On to the place where they will die.

18 Just like a little stream,
   As days and nights pass by,
   A person's goods are quickly finished,
   Life, furthermore, is transitory.

19 Nights are long when one can't sleep,
   The road seems long for those exhausted,
   The cyclic world is long also for those
   Who do not know the holy religion.

20 Thinking, 'I have a child and wealth'
   The infantile are ruined.
   Since in [or] out a self does not exist[8]
   What sense is there in 'my' child and 'my' wealth?

21 Even though they had everything in life,
   Many hundred thousand men
   And women from all walks of life
   Must go beneath the power of death.

22   Collections in the end disperse,
     Whatever rises must also fall.
     All meetings end in separation,
     The final end of life is death.

23   Since life at its end turns to death,
     All living beings, destined to die,
     Move ever closer to all those
     Results of good or bad they've done.

24   By doing bad [actions], people fall to hells;
     By virtue, rise to happy realms.
     Others meditate on the path and find
     Uncontaminated liberation.

25   Since Buddha and all the Hearers
     And all Solitary Realizers too,
     Give up the bodies that they have,
     It's definite that common folk do so too.

26   Wherever you go there is no place
     But that death can find an entry:
     Not earth, nor sky, nor ocean deep,
     Not far within the mountain side.

27   Seeing that everyone
     Who has been and is yet to be
     Gives up the body and departs,
     The wise have fear, follow religion,
         and lead pure lives.

28   Seeing old age and the pain of disease,
     And seeing the mind[9] depart at death,
     The steadfast give up the prison-like home
     That common people like and can't give up.

29   Even splendid royal coaches perish.
     Similarly bodies grow old.
     The holy Truth [Body] is holy,
     The best persons realize it and don't age.

30 Old age you are a horrid fool,
    And all the work you do is bad.
    You completely overcome
    The body that is beautiful.[10]

31 Those who have lived a hundred years
    Are led along by death himself.
    They either become old, or else
    Fall sick and are consumed by death.

32 Going ever on without return.
    Devastated as nights and days pass by,
    Having the pain of birth and death:
    It's like being a fish in a steaming pool.

33 Whether one sits or moves
    This life is irreversible,
    Just like a mighty river's course
    Going on and on both day and night.

34 Like fish inside a shallow pool,
    With the passing of each day and night
    This life becomes so very short —
    How can it be enjoyable?[11]

35 Since death will be the end of life
    This body grows completely old;
    It is a house of sickness that will crumble soon,
    A mass of gore that perishes.

36 Alas, unobstructed,[12] this body,
    Empty and without consciousness,
    Is thrown out like a blackened log
    That lies in a cremation ground.

37 It is right to give this body up,
    Full of pain and always sick,
    Tormented by old age and death
    And always leaking filthy stuff.

38   Use this gore-filled bag of bones
     That's soon to perish, often sick,
     To obtain accomplishments and bliss
     And peace without comparison.

39   When childish people think, 'I will
     Do this next summer or next spring
     Or when the winter comes around,'
     They do not see the hindrance.

40   Just like a flood passing through a town,
     Soon death arises and goes off
     With all the family, goods and wealth
     Of people whose minds still desire such things.

41   Your children cannot protect you when
     The time has come for you to die,
     Nor can your parents, nor your friends.
     You have no refuge at that time.

42   'When I've done this then I'll do that,
     And after that is finished, then I'll do this.'
     Old age, sickness, and death consume
     Those people who make such preparations.

43   So[13] always take joy in stability; placed
     In equipoise, make effort, look to the end
     Of life and death, completely crush all demon ranks.
     O monks! do this and transcend life and death.

2 Desire

1 Desires arise from [wrong] conceptions
So know them as desire's root.
Avoid conceptualizations
And then desire will not arise.

2 Lamenting arises from all desires,
From all desire comes fear,[14]
If all desire is given up
There is neither fear nor lamenting.

3 Lamenting arises from all pleasure,
From all pleasure comes fear,
If all pleasure is discarded
There is neither fear nor lamenting.

4 Desire and liking ripen into pain
Like sweetness that becomes a bitter taste,
Or like the torch not thrown away
That in the end burns the foolish holder.

5 Superiors say, 'Fetters
Of rope, or those of wood and iron
Are not as strong as attachments
To youths and jewelled earrings.'

6   They say, 'Although desire's bonds are loose
    It's hard to be completely free of them.'
    The steadfast spurn desire's happiness
    And cut them all and quickly flee.

7   The world in its variety is not desirable.
    It seems desirable through mental attraction.
    The steadfast subdue longing,
    Because the world remains in its variety.

8   They say, 'There is no permanent human desire,
    Whatever is desired is impermanent.
    So to end future birth, mentally
    Surrender them all and seek deathlessness.'

9   [They] say One Who Ascends has no
    Attachment to any object of desire,
    Does not long for and contaminate [objects][15]
    And [has] a fault-free mind and memory.

10 A wise person is like a silversmith
    And gradually, step by step,
    Refines and purifies the mind
    Of even the smallest impurity.

11 Like a cobbler who first cures
    The leather, then makes it into shoes,
    There is a complete happiness
    With the abandoning of each desire.

12 If you desire every joy,
    Completely forsake all desire.
    By forsaking completely all desire
    A most excellent ecstasy is found.

13 So long as [you] follow desire
    Satisfaction is never found.
    Whoever reverses desire,
    With wisdom, attains satisfaction.

14   So satisfaction is precluded by desire
     While wisdom gives rise to contentment.
     All those whom wisdom satisfies
     Don't fall beneath the power of craving.[16]

15   Alas! Whoever longs for [objects of] desire
     Enjoys [doing] what is not religious.
     While there is just a bit of life
     [They] do not see the hindrance.

16   The vile are overcome by pleasure
     And do not try to go beyond.
     Debased, the craving for desires
     Brings harm to themselves and others.

17   Even though a rain of *kārshāpaṇa*[17] falls
     The greedy are not satisfied.
     The wise are sure that great harm comes
     From even very faint desire.

18   To Buddhas and the Hearers
     Who take no pleasure in even
     The objects that the gods desire,
     The end of craving gives pleasure.

19   They understand that even a heap of gold
     As big as a high snow mountain
     Cannot satisfy even one person,
     And therefore conduct themselves well.

20   Those who know this cause of misery
     Never take pleasure in desires.
     Seeing the causes of pain in all worlds
     They practise steadily to pacify them all.

3 Craving

1 Completely overcome by [wrong] conception
People develop irresistible attachments
And see [objects] as clean; the objects of
Attachment increase and their bonds ensnare them.

2 Those who enjoy calming wrong conception,
Always mindful to meditate
On ugliness, loosen their bonds
By completely giving up their craving.

3 All those enveloped by the net of murky desire,
Covered by craving's covering,
Careless and ensnared by bonds
Are like fish in a boiling pool.[18]

4 Craving grows like a vine[19]
When people act without any caution.
They follow after old age and death
Like suckling calves wanting their mother's milk.

5 Those who remember and cling to objects
And pine for mental happiness,
Wander in the cycle of life and death continuously
Like monkeys in an orchard after fruit.

6   Those who always desire pleasure
    Become closer to birth and old age.
    Beings led on by their craving
    Are like rabbits struggling in a trap.

7   All those tied up by craving's knot
    Grow attached to real or unreal things,
    Infants[19a] enjoying the taste of clasps[20]
    Will meet misery again and again.

8   Those without accomplishments and bliss,
    Involved in doing the demon's work,
    Follow after their old age and death
    Like suckling calves wanting their mother's milk.

9   Through this [teaching], having given up
       such yearnings,
    And freed from craving real or unreal things,
    Monks who eclipse all existences
    Achieve non-residual nirvana.

10 Commanded by this sexual craving
    So hard for worldly beings to cast away,
    A person's pain increases
    Like weeds when rain has fallen.

11 Having cast away, like dew-drops from
    A lotus flower in bloom, this sexual craving,
    So hard for worldly beings to cast away,
    A person's pains are stopped.[21]

12 Therefore, you who have come are being told
    To be as happy as you can.
    Like weeds around an *uśīra* plant
    Pull out all craving by its root.

13 Since those who make friends with craving
    Wander for ages [through the world],
    Completely uproot craving:
    Then there is neither pain nor fear.

14   Again and again they take birth,
     Again and again they enter wombs.
     First here, then elsewhere for awhile
     Beings come and then wander on.

15   Give up craving so hard to cast away
     And kill its seed here through this [teaching].
     Those without craving do not
     Go through the cycle [of birth and death] again.

16   Don't waste the opportunity.
     Born as human or god
     One exists in thrall to yearning.
     Rise above craving for objects.

17   Those who are born in hells
     Regret their wasted opportunity.
     Therefore unless one pacifies
     The craving for objects — cause of the sea of life,
     The basis of [bad] fruit, the tormentor
     That spreads a net of creeping vines —
     Continually arising misery
     Can never be completely stopped.

18   Though cut, a tree not torn out by the root
     Will simply grow again.
     Likewise, recurring misery is not dislodged
     Unless afflictive craving is torn out.

19   As with a weapon I myself have made
     Used by robbers to murder me,
     The craving that comes from within
     Is what takes my life.

20   So having understood the fault
     Of craving that brings forth pain,
     Give it up. Then there is no attachment[22]
     And [one] is a mindful monk[23] in all things.

4 *Caution*

1 Caution (*apramāda, bag yod*) is the ground of immortality
  Carelessness the ground of death.
  With caution death does not occur,
  With carelessness there is always death.

2 When they understand this difference
  All wise persons are cautious.
  The ecstasy in being cautious
  Is the pleasure known by Superiors.

3 Constantly meditating on this point,
  Always subduing the other side,
  The steadfast encounter bliss and power
  And incomparable nirvana.

4 When wise persons overturn
  Carelessness with their caution,
  They arrive at wisdom's mansion
  And free of pain, kindly and steadfast,
  Survey from the mountain top,
  The child-like people on the ground.

5 With effort and with caution,

Pure morality and calm,
The wise become as islands
And turn back the great rivers.[24]

6   Wide spreads the fame of all who are cautious,
Who persevere and have remembrance,
Good conduct, thoughtful activity
Pure vows and a religious way of life.

7   Be concerned with the surpassing mind,
Training on all the bases of the Kings.[25]
Nirvana is the protection
Of those who always remember peace.

8   Don't have an inferior religion,
Growing familiar with carelessness.
Don't have a liking for wrong views.
Do not increase the world.

9   Anyone be they great or small
Who holds the perfect worldly[26] view
Does not migrate to lower realms
In a thousand future lives.

10   Infantile beings are those
Who are careless and ruin themselves.
The wise are prudent people
Like merchants who protect their goods.

11   Those who do not become careless,
Letting love for desires grow,
Who always think cautiously
Attain the end of contamination.

12   Though contamination's end is not gained
Do not be careless at this time.
Like the lion by the female beast
All those who are careless are killed.[27]

13   Four things beset careless people
Who go off with someone else's spouse:

They gain no merit, do not sleep in peace,
Third [they] are despised and fourth [they]
  go to hell.
They do wrong, no merit is attained,
Worry and fear accompany slight bliss,
Then sentenced to death by the great king
They're hanged and boil in the living hells.

14 All those who want personal happiness
    Act [with caution] as [taught] above.
    Steadfast ones do not become
    Like an infant's cart and meander off.

15 When, for example, the infant's cart
    Turns from the well-kept thoroughfares
    On to rough streets, the axles break
    And there is great sadness.
    Likewise, infants who give up
    Dharma and engage in wrong
    Fall beneath the power of death
    And like the broken axle are smashed.

16 Contamination increases for those who,
    Confident in carelessness,
    Have given up the work
    And do all that ought not be done.
    Those whose contamination has increased
    Recede from the uncontaminated.

17 Those mindful of the body nature[28]
    Who always undertake what is good,
    Continually doing the work,
    Avoiding what ought not be done,
    Aware and with remembrance
    Will end all contamination.
    Those who have ended contamination
    Gain the uncontaminated.

Those who just talk a lot
Are not holding holy Dharma.

18   Those who take heed of the teaching
And physically actualize
The little bit that they have heard
Are holding the holy Dharma.

19   Although they may speak much that's true,
Like shepherds counting someone else's sheep
The careless, not doing what they preach,
Don't amass the fortune of religious work.

20   Although they may speak but little of the truth,
Those who practise what the doctrine says
And give up hate, desire, and ignorance
Find the fortune of religious work.

21   By singing caution's constant praise
And criticizing carelessness,
Caution becomes, among the gods,
More important than a hundred offerings,

22   Whether they do the work or not[29]
The wise sing caution's praise.
The wise and prudent ones
Attain both aims with complete ease.

23   In this way they realize
The aims of this life
And the aims of future lives also;
They are referred to as 'the wise.'

24   The monks, enjoying caution
And viewing carelessness with fear,
Pull themselves out from lower realms,
Like an elephant from the mud.

25   The monks, enjoying caution
     And viewing carelessness with fear
     Shake off all that is wrong
     Like wind shakes off the leaves from trees.

26   The monks, enjoying caution
     And viewing carelessness with fear
     Deal with afflictions both coarse and fine,
     Just like the burning of a fire.

27   The monks, enjoying caution
     And viewing carelessness with fear
     Gradually experience
     Freedom from every affliction.

28   The monks, enjoying caution
     And viewing carelessness with fear
     Pacify the composites
     And realize each state of peace.[30]

29   The monks, enjoying caution
     And viewing carelessness with fear
     Will not degenerate because
     They are close to nirvana.[31]

30   Those who with effort and caution
     Do religious work — do good —
     By their religious work attain
     Pleasure in this life and beyond.

31   For peace rely on the trainings,
     Be enthusiastic and try hard.
     Realize, everyone, that forgetfulness,
     Carelessness and weak endeavours,
     Not keeping vows and sleepiness,
     A scattered mind and laziness
     Are dangerous to the trainings,
     And don't squander that remembrance.

32   By keeping pure morality
     And taking pleasure in caution,
     O monks, rest in all-knowing equipoise
     And take good care of your minds.

33   Get to work and get away,
     Engage yourself in what the Buddha said;
     Like elephants do to mud houses,
     Overcome the ranks of death.

34   All who conduct themselves with caution
     In this religion of calming,
     Abandon the cycle of births
     And make an end of misery.

5 *Beauty*

1 Sorrows arise from all beauty
   From all beauty arises fear.
   When all beauty is given up
   Neither sorrow nor fear exists.

2 Sorrows arise from prettiness,
   From the pretty, misery and fear;
   When all that prettiness changes,
   Despondency arises.

3 Every worldly type of misery,
   Each anguished sorrowful lament
   Arises contingent upon beauty.
   When beauty is given up they arise no more.

4 There is happiness and no sorrow
   In those places on earth where beauty has been
      forsaken.
   So those who seek freedom from dust and pain
   Are never concerned with beauty.

5 Beauty not seen brings misery
Just as when ugliness is seen.
Therefore do not involve yourself
With beauty or even with ugliness.

6 Separation from beauty
And meeting with ugliness
Gives sorrow that is unbearable
To people who are getting old.

7 When someone beautiful dies,
The sorrow of intimate friends
And family lasts very long.
Parting from beauty brings misery.

8 When ugliness and beauty are no more
Bonds to them are not found.
Therefore don't treat as beautiful,
Beauty that has defilement.

9 Those who forsake their goals for beauty
Do not engage in what brings pleasure;
They do what brings unhappiness
Yet wish those acts would bring pleasure.[32]

10 Those captivated by the pleasure
Of comely shapes, do wrong,
Sink from the state of human or god
And go under the power of age and death.

11 The cautious who both day and night
Abandon comely shapes, give up
That demon-food[33] that's hard to leave
And extirpate the root of wrongs.

12 Treating ugliness as beauty
And that which is not good as good,
Treating what is misery as bliss
Those without caution are destroyed.

13   If one has concern for oneself,
     And does wrong, one does not
     Attain an easy happiness,
     So do not pursue beauty[34] here.

14   If one has concern for oneself
     And does good, then, one simply
     Attains an easy happiness.
     So do not pursue wrong doing here.

15   Just as remote settlements
     Surround themselves with secure moats,
     If one has liking for oneself
     Keep a guard here guarding carefully.

16   The concerned person,
     Being intelligent, is a
     Sentinel at all three times
     And keeps the guard guarding carefully.

17   Just as the remote settlements
     Protect themselves inside and out,
     Similarly protect yourself;
     Don't waste this perfect human birth.

18   Besides taking rebirth in hell
     One's life is squandered and one feels regret.

19   Though searching all directions with my mind
     I see none with more beauty than myself.
     Since others also [see] themselves as beautiful,
     Therefore I do not harm others.

20   Since everyone holds life
     Most dear and fears its loss,
     Consider how you hold yourself
     And do not strike or kill.

21 The gods extol the virtues
    Of those beings with good conduct;
    None disparages them here
    And they attain the bliss of heaven.[35]

22 Just as a family and friends
    Sing out for joy when they see
    A long lost exiled relative
    Coming without mishap from afar,
    So those who have merit feel joy
    As for a relative, at the approach
    Of people who have made merits
    As they go through this world.

23 So collect together merit
    For what lies beyond this world;
    Beyond this world merits become
    The ground of every living being.[36]

24 Dharma practice [kindness], complete morality,
    Awareness and a sense of shame,
    And truthful speech does my own work
    And causes others happiness.[37]

25 I undertake my purpose
    And other beings become happy;
    In this life there is praise,
    And a happy rebirth in the next.

26 Holy beings feel happiness
    When incorrect conduct is stopped;
    Those beings who are not holy do not [feel happiness]
    When taught [ethics], and told the inner [work].

27 So the excellent and the not-excellent ·
    Are separated at their death;
    Those not holy go to hell,
    The holy beings proceed to high states.

6 *Ethics*

1 Among seekers of the three happinesses —
The happiness of compliments,
Of getting wealth, and of an upper birth —
Those who are wise protect ethics.

2 The wise who also see the ground[38]
Of Superiors — the ground of complete seeing,
And of the basis of calming
This world — protect ethics.

3 From ethics happiness is gained,
There are no physical torments,
At night a peaceful sleep,
And happiness on waking up.[39]

4 Benevolent and ethical,
With the merits from what they do,
The wise always find happiness
Here and in the beyond.

5 Ethics are a virtue even in old age,
And to remain faithful is good.
Widsom is the jewel of the human race
And thieves find merit hard to steal.

6   Monks abiding in ethics,
    Who also restrain their senses
    And know the measure of a meal,
    And try to stay awake,
    Never completely degenerate.
    By their efforts in these areas
    And not being lazy day or night,
    They get closer to nirvana.

7   Monks who are ethical
    And strive at the meditations
    On mind and wisdom —
    They will obtain the end of misery.

8   Therefore always have each mindfulness,
    Awareness, and the guarding
    Of ethics and stability,
    And the practice of insight.

9   After affliction is ended by these,
    Parting from mind[40] and ending the rest occurs.
    Those with wisdom whose bodies have perished
    Thus pass to infinite nirvana.

10 Those who have meditated well
    On ethics, wisdom and stability,
    Reaching the extremely stainless end,
    Have no more pain. They end future births
    And being freed from the bonds of grasping
    Give up the body. With their wisdom
    They go beyond the demon's land
    And shine out radiant like the sun.[41]

11 Those monks, carelessly self-assured
    About inner and outer things
    Do not become fully perfect
    In ethics, wisdom and stability.

12 Rain does not fall from a clear sky;
    Rain falls from the cover of clouds.
    So clear away the covering clouds
    And then the rain will not fall.[42]

13 Similarly always be watching
    And keep the ethics of the ordained,
    And quickly make immaculate
    The path that leads to liberation.

14 The fragrances of flowers, joss-sticks, herbs
    And sandalwood don't move without a breeze.
    Holy fragrance is not diffused by wind
    For the fragrance of the holy spreads everywhere.

15 The sweet fragrance of ethics transcends
    That of every kind of incense:
    Of joss-sticks and of sandalwood,
    Of myrrh[43] and blue water lilies.

16 The sweet fragrance of sandalwood
    And joss-sticks lasts but briefly here;
    That imbued with the sweet fragrance
    Of ethics, spreads here and into heaven.

17 Therefore being cautious,
    Achieve immaculate ethics.
    When perfect wisdom sets one free
    The path of demons is not found.

18 This is the path to happiness,
    It is the purifying path;
    Engaging in it meditate,
    And abandon the demon's bonds.

7 *Fine Conduct*

1 Keeping fine physical conduct
And giving up conduct that is wrong,
One guards against great physical wrongdoing
And the body becomes controlled.

2 By keeping fine verbal conduct
And giving up conduct that is wrong,
One guards against the wrongdoing of speech
And the speech becomes controlled.

3 By keeping fine mental conduct
And giving up conduct that is wrong,
One guards against the wrongdoing of mind
And the mind becomes controlled.

4 Give up bad physical conduct
And verbal conduct that is bad.
Give up bad mental conduct too
And any other of one's faults.

5 Do every physical virtue, and
Virtues of speech both great and small.
Do every virtuous mental act

And possess the four immeasurables.[44]
If all physical virtue is done
And speech and mind do virtue too,
In this and all your future lives
You always attain happiness.

6   Since they are always physically controlled
The Mighty[45] do no harm.[46]
They go to immortality
Where sorrow is not found.

7   Since they always control their words
The Mighty do no harm.
They go to immortality
Where sorrow is not found.

8   Since they always control their minds
The Mighty do no harm.
They go to immortality
Where sorrow is not found.

9   Since the Steadfast[47] are physically controlled
And since they have control
Over their speech and minds,
Since they retain complete control
They go to immortality
Where sorrow is not found.

10   Physical control is good,
And good, as well, control of speech.
Control of mind is also good
And good is control in everything:
That person who is fully controlled
Finds freedom from all misery.

11   Guarding your speech, controlling well your mind,
Doing no physical non-virtues:
If these three action-paths are practised
You find the path of which the Sage has sung.

8 *Words*

1 Whoever says that happened which in fact did not,
   And all those who lie, descend to hell.
   When they go beyond, both are alike
   In having degraded qualities.

2 Foul words, issuing from
   The mouths of living beings
   Become a verbal axe
   With which those beings cut themselves.

3 Praising those who should be despised
   And censuring who should be praised,
   Storing up quarrels with their mouths,
   The quarrelsome do not find happiness.

4 Quarrels of those who lose their wealth at dice
   Are settled up here for just a trifle.
   But those enraged at a One Gone Thus
   Have picked a huge quarrel for life.

5 Because mind and speech are superior,
   Scorn sends one for ten million[48]
   And forty-one thousand years to cold hells
   Called blistering and burst-blister hells.

6 With a wicked mind, insulting the faultless
   Just kills oneself and increases hell.
   The faultless powerful ones are patient,
   They do not even feel annoyed.

7 Because of their evil belief,
   Those beings who lose their temper
   Forsake what is superior —
   Foe Destroyers, teaching and religious life —
   And like the bamboo gone to seed
   Are destroyed by their fruit.

8 When speaking, speak only good words;
   Do not say anything wicked.
   It is better to speak good words
   Than wickedness which causes pain.

9 The infants who speak wickedly
   Become fettered when they talk.
   Superiors don't say these things
   Which, if uttered, give up another [good birth].

10 The monks' speech is controlled,
   Precise and without haughtiness.

11 Whoever teaches religion's meaning
   Speaks pleasingly. Superiors speak
   The best eloquence,
   Their speech is pleasant and not harsh,
   True not false, and
   Is religious not vulgar speech.

12 These are the words to speak;
   Utter elequently these words
   Which bring neither pain to yourself
   Nor cause another person harm.

13 Speak only those pleasant words
   Which bring enjoyment to the one who hears,
   Which create joy,
   And which do not generate wrong.

14   True words are heavenly nectar
     For true words reign supreme.
     That grounded in religion and facts
     Is called 'truth' by the holy beings.

15   Supreme among all words
     Are those the Buddha speaks
     To eliminate all misery —
     True words which go beyond sorrow.

9 *Actions*

1 Transgressing that one value
   That loses the next world,
   There then remains no single wrong
   The liar will not do.

2 Better to eat
   A piece of food like molten iron
   Than to eat alms from the public
   As a hypocrite not keeping vows.

3 If you are scared of misery
   And if you do not relish pain
   Do not do secretly or openly
   What wicked people do.

4 If you have done something wrong
   Or are involved in wrong
   And run away hoping to hide the fact,
   It is no use; there is no escape.
   There exists no place at all
   But what you have done will follow you:
   In the oceans, through the skies,
   Or far off in mountain caves.

 5 Do not do the bad actions
    You discover that others do —
    Do not do those things;
    The wrongs you do will follow you.

 6 Extremely violent acts, deceit
    And swindling on weight and bulk,
    Doing harm to other beings,
    And enciting others to these wrongs:
    The consequences of these actions
    Hurl the one who does them from the cliff.

 7 Whether it was good or bad,
    The power of any action
    Once performed is never lost;
    The results arise accordingly.

 8 While that collection [of virtue] remains
    This one gives torment [to you].
    Consider these torments
    Which other tormenters will give
      [if you ruin them].[49]

 9 Infants say of the unconsidered wrong they do,
    'There is no consequence.'
    Those who migrate due to wrong action
    Will understand [this] in future lives.

10 Being without understanding,
    Each bad action that infants do
    Delivers its burning result
    At an appropriate time.

11 It is your own actions that later on
    Bring torment like a searing flame.

12 Unintelligent infantile beings
    Treat themselves like enemies.
    They do all the wrong actions
    Which bring painful results.

13   Better to refrain from actions
     Which ripen into resulting
     Misery and a veil of tears
     That shroud the weeping face.

14   Better to perform actions
     Which do not cause misery
     And which ripen into results
     Of mental happiness and joy.

15   One will experience with tears
     The fruition of each wrong action
     That, wanting personal happiness,
     One did with laughter.

16   Like milk [turning to curd], a definite bad deed
     Does not cause change at once.
     Like fire concealed beneath the ash
     It burns infant-like beings.

17   Wrong actions do not necessarily
     Cut immediately like swords.
     Those who migrate through wrong actions
     Actualize the result afterwards.

18   Those who migrate through wrong actions
     Realize in a future life
     Every painful fruition
     Of their previous perverted deeds.

19   As rust forms on a piece of iron
     And then corrodes that iron away,
     Likewise through your thoughtless action
     You go to a bad migration.

10 *Faith*

1 The holy beings praise faith, and shame,
  Ethics and benevolence.[50]
  They say, 'With these one treads
  The path leading to the celestial world.'

2 Misers don't migrate to celestial worlds.
  Being infants, they don't praise benevolence.
  The steadfast who rejoice in benevolence
  Experience joy in other lives.

3 It has been said, 'Best of all tastes is truth,[51]
  Living by wisdom the best of lives.
  In this life humanity's finest jewel is faith.
  Joy is gained here by religion.'[52]

4 By generating faith in the Foe Destroyer's
  Religion which goes to nirvana,
  The wise listen with reverence[53]
  And gain the wisdom of that and that.

5 With caution find freedom from the seas.
  With faith find freedom from the rivers.
  With effort eliminate misery,
  And with wisdom become completely pure.[54]

6 Monks who make a friend of faith,
  Who are led along by intelligence
  And strongly want nirvana
  Sever all the binding ropes.

7 The wise who give up all faults
  By a fine familiarity with faith,
  Ethics and intelligence are said to have
  The finest way of being faithful.

8 Offerings are made to those
  With faith and excellent ethics;
  Benevolent and freed from miserliness,
  In each and every place they go.

9 The wise take faith and intelligence
  For their security in life;
  These are their finest wealth.
  That other wealth is just commonplace.

10 Those who want superior ideas,
  Who like to listen to doctrine,
  And those freed from stains of avarice
  Are those 'who have faith'.[53]

11 Take the provisions of the path of faith,
  Which thieves of wealth cannot devour.
  Stop the stealing of the thieves.
  Religious beings take this up with joy.
  Always feel happiness for the
  Approach of wise religious beings.

12 A benefactor, out of faith,
  Gives whatever possible of food
  And drink to other beings.
  Anyone who feels upset by that
  Does not achieve stability
  Of mind by night or day.

13 Whoever cuts off such [envy],
  Like cutting the palmyra tree bud,

Achieves stability of mind
Throughout day and night.

14 Do not rely on faithless people
Who are like dried-up springs,
Or if water yet bubbles out,
Give forth a putrid, stagnant smell.

15 The intelligent rely on those with faith,
Just as those who want water find
A lake that is both deep and clear,
Soothing and without turbulence.

16 Though neither love nor lack of love
Directs a Conqueror's gaze,
The Victor abandons those without faith
And teaches to those who are faithful.

11 *The Ordained Person*

1 [True] Brahmins fully forsake desire,
  With effort they cut the stream [of birth];
  Without fully forsaking desire
  The Conqueror [state] is not attained.

2 Inferior itinerants[56]
  Again amass afflictions in the future.
  So always do this specific task[57]
  With unremitting steady work.

3 All the inferior actions,
  All completely afflictive austerities,
  And what is not perfect pure conduct
  Seem meaningful but are not so.

4 Just as an arrow held wrongly
  Injures a person's hand,
  So too, guarding badly
  Religious behavior leads one to hell.

5 Just as an arrow held properly
  Does not injure a person's hand,
  So too, properly guarding [vows]
  Lifts the ordained person beyond pain.

6 For weak, remorseful beings
   Who don't know what religious behaviour involves,
   Transcendence and patience are hard
   And many miseries arise.

7 Without continual remorse,[58]
   And without removing the misconception
   Under which the mind labours,
   How can religious work be done?

8 Ordained ones who are bad, liking bad things,
   Who stay at home, undertaking wrong[59]
   Cleave to unequalled misery
   And just store up the sorrow of rebirth.

9 Most persons who wear saffron robes
   Don't keep perfect ordination.
   The bad like [to teach] what is bad
   And wicked, and go to lower realms.

10 Like vines around a *sāla* tree
   All those with crooked ethics
   Manage to treat themselves
   Just as an enemy would do.

11 Someone's hair merely turning to grey
   Does not class that person among the venerable.[60]
   Virility having come to an end,
   A person is said to be simply senile.

12 The virtuous who give up wrongs
   And practise in a pure way,
   Who work, free from the [future] crowd,[61]
   They are known as 'venerable'.

13 A liar who does not keep morality
   Is just someone bald without religion.
   How can a fool running after desires
   Ever really be religious?

14 A liar who does not keep morality

Is just someone bald without religion.
The wise know those who stop doing
All wrongs are religious.[62]

15 A liar who does not keep morality
Is just someone bald without religion.
Those who fully identify
All gross and subtle immorality
And stop doing all wrong —
They are called true religious persons.

16 A Brahmin is one freed from wrongs;[63]
Someone with ordination vows,
Completely freed from stains of self:
This one is called an 'ordained person'.

12 *The Path*

1 At the time that wisdom sees
   The four truths of Superiors,
   This path is fully understood[64]
   And craving for existence fully cut.

2 Just as a shower of rain settles
   Dust blown up by the wind,
   When wisdom sees, then
   Conceptualizations are calmed down.

3 'The foremost' is worldly wisdom[65]
   Which is a definite bringer [of the path]:
   The fine realization by which
   The end of birth and death emerges.

4 Among all truths stand these four truths;
   Among all paths this eightfold noble path;
   Among the living the best is one who sees;
   Abandoning desire the best religion.

5 At the time when wisdom sees
   That compounds are impermanent,
   The mind renounces misery,
   The path becomes purified.

6   At the time when wisdom sees
    That compounds are in essence empty
    The mind renounces misery,
    The path becomes purified.

7   At the time when wisdom sees
    That compounds are without a self
    The mind renounces misery,
    And the path becomes purified.

8   As One Gone Thus and Teacher
    The path that I am teaching you
    Severs the pain of not knowing.
    You are the ones who must do it.

9   As One Gone Thus and Teacher
    The path that I am teaching you
    Excludes the pain of [all] craving.
    You are the ones who must do it.

10 There being no other path than this
    To purify [wrong] view [of self]
    Stay well in stabilization
    And throw off the demon's bonds.

11 This true surpassing single way
    Like a swan's unwavering flight onto a lake,
    The Buddha realized in equipoise
    And explained repeatedly to groups.
    The One who knows the end of birth and death,
    The Helper, out of love, teaches
    This single path by which all the waters
    Were and will be and are being crossed.

12 He who sees all teaches well this path
    For the final stage, peace and purity,
    To end the round of birth and death
    And give full knowledge in all spheres.

13 Just as the stream of the river Gaṅgā goes,
    Flows down and merges in the sea,

The path taught by [the One with] broad wisdom
Is entered to attain the state of deathlessness.

14   I prostrate to Him who passed from existence,
That Refuge who pacifies gods and humans,
Who out of loving-kindness for all beings
Turned the wheel of the then unheard Dharma.[66]

15   In guarding the three virtuous conceptions,
Eliminate the three non-virtuous ones.
As a shower settles the blowing dust,
Pacify rough and subtle conception.[67]
Then conception is calmed in the mind
And the bliss of unsurpassed enlightenment[68] is
    touched.

16   Turning the mind to the three stabilizations,[69]
Meditate on the immeasurables born from truth.[70]
Mindful wise ones pacify the demons
And cut off the three places with these three.[71]

17   With the sword of wisdom, the strength of effort,
Remembrance, equipoise and joy in stability,
The arising and perishing of the world is seen
And liberation from all is known.
The last world is fully realized
And [when that is] left behind,
[The state attained is] called 'gone beyond'.

18   By this meditating on the calm,
True, superior eightfold path
Nectar is found, fame increases,
And longed-for happiness and praise attained.

Folio Two

13 *Honours*

1 Like the womb of the female mule,
   Like the bamboo, and plantain fruit
   By which the sources are themselves destroyed,
   Honours disrupt the weak.

2 The foolish are completely ruined
   As long as they are offered honours.
   The infant's white part[72] becomes obscured,
   That person's level also surely declines.

3 Vile beings who want material wealth,
   The monks who want a retinue,
   Those who are greedy for a place,
   Those [wanting] gifts from lineage other [than family],
   And those who trick either the ordained
   Or laity [into honouring] them,
   Thinking, 'I want them in my power
   To do or not do work' —
   The greed increases in the minds
   Of infants harbouring such ideas.
   'The way of getting rich differs
   From that by which nirvana is attained.'

4 Having seen what is meant by this,
   Monks who are Buddhist Hearers
   Take no pleasure in honours,
   And gradually increase detachment.[73]

5 Don't seek anything at all,
   Don't trick any person [into honouring you].
   Shun other manner of life,
   Don't treat religion like a trade.

6 Use those things that are given to you;
   Don't covet what your neighbour has.
   Monks who covet others' goods
   Fail to achieve stabilization.

7 If you want to live a happy life[74]
   And view [things] as a religious person,[75]
   Enjoy the clothes and food and drink
   Given to you as community.

8 If you want to live a happy life
   And view [things] as a religious person,
   Huddle in your pure sleeping place
   Like a snake in a mouse's hole.

9 If you want to live a happy life
   And view [things] as a religious person,
   Content yourself with meagre things
   And focus on one-pointedness.[76]

10 Although many are unaware that
    One keeps good ethics and equipoise,[77]
    Those who know this give praise, saying,
    'This one lives purely and is not lazy.'

11 Thinking, 'This person does not know a thing,'
    Fools can even abuse someone holding
    The three uncontaminated knowledges[78]
    That overcome the Lord of Death.

12   [These fools] offer to people
     Who have defilement
     And who possess [much] food and drink
     That which they [themselves] have been given.

13   Tonsured infants in saffron robes
     Want food and drink,
     Rich clothes and bedding:
     They just find themselves more enemies.

14   Although food will not pacify the mind,
     To keep alive, do not give up eating.
     Go beg for alms, realizing that food
     Will keep the body healthy and alive.

15   Having realized the harm
     Of these terrifying honours,
     There is less trickery, a relaxed mind,
     Mindfulness, ordination, and the full going.[79]

16   The homage and offerings by those of good lineage
     Are like a subtle pain[80] that's hard to cure;
     The honours [that the foolish] can't resist
     Should be realized to be like mud.

14   *Animosity*

1   Having animosity
    Toward those who have done no wrong,
    Taints all infantile beings[81]
    In this and in the future world.

2   First it ruins me, and then
    Later ruins others as well,
    Like birds used as falcon bait
    Ruined and ruining others too.

3   By striking, one is struck.
    By enmity, one finds those with enmity.
    So too, by abuse one is abused.
    Animosity breeds animosity.

4   Unlike the religious person,[82] infants
    Unskilled in the holy Dharma
    Feel enmity over trifles
    Even though life is very short.

5   Having thought, 'This [reconciliation] is the best,'[85]
    [The wise] reconcile the arguments
    [That arise] when community is divided

Through lack of power [of insight] and thought;
The wise speak considered words.
[The laity] become reconciled
After battery and murder,
Cattle rustling and robbery,
Even destruction of countries.
If you understand this religion
Which teaches the object — [the close mindfulness]
Why don't you [the ordained] act likewise?

6 The system [of you who argue] is not skilled.
The others do not understand
Because you are talking nonsense:
Therefore I am trying [to teach] this [Buddhist way].

7 Those who are skilled at this [teaching]
Calm the [others] with the appropriate words:
'One is talking to and abusing oneself,
Engineering one's own defeat.'

8 'Whoever becomes offended
Will never pacify enmity.
One is talking to and abusing oneself,
Engineering one's own defeat.
Whoever does not take offense
Will pacify enmity.
Here [in this world] enmity will never pacify
Those who bear you enmity.[84]
Patience pacifies enmity —
That is the nature of Dharma.'[85]

9 Enmity never calms those with enmity;
Those without enmity calm enmity down.
Since bearing resentment harms other beings,
The wise do not feel enmity.

10 If you find a firm, well-grounded
Skilful friend with whom to work,
Suppress every affliction
And work mindfully with a happy heart.

11   If you don't find a firm, well-grounded,
     Skilful friend with whom to work,
     Work alone doing no wrong, like the king[86]
     Who gives up his lands and retinue.

12   If you don't find a wholesome friend
     With whom you work in harmony
     Don't befriend the infantile.
     Work on steadily alone.

13   Do not befriend infant-like ones,
     Working alone is easier.
     Like the Matang elephant,[87]
     Work alone with a relaxed mind.[88]

15 *Mindfulness*

1 As Buddha has taught, from fully
   Completed fine meditation
   On mindfulness of breathing in and out,
   Gradually an emergence occurs,
   Which like the unclouded sun and moon
   Illuminates the entire world.

2 If, when standing, sitting, and at rest,
   Body and likewise mind are positioned,
   And mindfulness well placed [on breathing],
   The monk will attain all the stages.[89]
   If all the stages come to be attained
   Not even the King of Death will find [the practitioner].

3 After positioning close mindfulness
   On the body, whoever then controls
   The six sources of contact and always remains
   In equipoise, will realize nirvana.

4 Those who always position close mindfulness
   On the body in all of its aspects[90]
   Do not adhere to 'self' nor to 'mine';
   No adherance to self or mine will arise.

Therefore monks in such equipoise
Quickly transcend all craving for objects.

5 Those who are sentries[91] and work at Dharma
With mindfulness, awareness, equipoise,
Joy and great faith at the [right] times
Will, it is said, transcend birth and old age.

6 Always relying on such sentry duty,
Wise bhikshus with mindfulness and effort
Give up clasping to all births
And attain liberation in this [life].

7 Listen to me! you on sentry duty,
Wakers-up of those who sleep,
Being a sentry is easier than sleeping —
There are no fears on sentry duty.[92]

8 By persevering at this sentry duty,
Always practising day and night
And admiring deathlessness greatly,
All contamination comes to an end.

9 Whoever has recollection
Of the Buddha all day and night
Has taken refuge in the Buddha
And makes the discovery desired by the living.[93]

10 Whoever has recollection
Of the Dharma all day and night
Has taken refuge in the Dharma
And makes the discovery desired by the living.

11 Whoever has recollection
Of the Community all day and night
Has taken refuge in the Community
And makes the discovery desired by the living.

12 Whoever has recollection
Of the Buddha all day and night
Is a Hearer of Gautama
Because [that one is] woken up, wide awake.[94]

13 Whoever has recollection
    Of the Dharma all day and night
    Is a Hearer of Gautama
    Because [that one is] woken up, wide awake.

14 Whoever has recollection
    Of the Community all day and night
    Is a Hearer of Gautama
    Because [that one is] woken up, wide awake.[95]

15 Whoever has recollection
    Of ethics all day and night
    Is a Hearer of Gautama
    Because [that one is] woken up, wide awake.[96]

16 Whoever has recollection
    Of generosity all day and night
    Is a Hearer of Gautama
    Because [that one is] woken up, wide awake.[97]

17 Whoever has recollection
    Of the gods all day and night
    Is a Hearer of Gautama
    Because [that one is] woken up, wide awake.[98]

18 Whoever is always mindful
    Of the body all day and night
    Is a Hearer of Gautama
    Because [that one is] woken up, wide awake.[99]

19 Whoever is always mindful
    Of the four stabilizations all day and night
    Is a Hearer of Gautama
    Because [that one is] woken up, wide awake.[100]

20 The one whose mind takes joy
    In not doing harm all day and night
    Is a Hearer of Gautama
    Because [that one is] woken up, wide awake.[101]

21 The one whose mind takes joy
    In not thinking harm all day and night

Is a Hearer of Gautama
Because [that one is] woken up, wide awake.[102]

22   The one whose mind takes joy
In meditating all day and night
Is a Hearer of Gautama
Because [that one is] woken up, wide awake.[103]

23   The one whose mind takes joy
In emptiness, all day and night
Is a Hearer of Gautama
Because [that one is] woken up, wide awake.[104]

24   The one whose mind takes joy
In signlessness all day and night
Is a Hearer of Gautama
Because [that one is] woken up, wide awake.

25   The one whose mind takes joy
In nothingness all day and night
Is a Hearer of Gautama
Because [that one is] woken up, wide awake.[105]

26   The one whose mind takes joy
In definite emergence all day and night
Is a Hearer of Gautama
Because [that one is] woken up, wide awake.[106]

27   The one whose mind takes joy
In detachment all day and night
Is a Hearer of Gautama
Because [that one is] woken up, wide awake.

28   The one whose mind takes joy
In nirvana all day and night
Is a Hearer of Gautama
Because [that one is] woken up, wide awake.

16 *Miscellaneous*

1 Do sentry work, one's task, at the outset
   Because the time for work reverts.[107]

2 When first you have done like this —
   Seen the task, and the time for work, and want to end
   [Misery], since you have beheld that the practice
   [Brings] what is desired —
   You should therefore concentrate until
   The purpose is fully attained,
   And by concentration and fortitude
   Become an island unto yourself.

3 Purify all of your stains
   Like a silversmith does silver.
   Cleansed of stains, no faults[108] arise;
   Birth and death no longer arise.

4 Motivated by their wrong views —
   Ashamed when shame need not be felt
   And not ashamed of shameful things,
   Afraid of what is not fearful
   And unafraid of the fearful —
   The living migrate to lower realms.

5 Those who first are careless in this Dharma practice,
   Then later on become cautious,
   Illuminate the entire world
   Just as the unclouded sun and moon.

6 Those who first are careless in this,
   Then later on become cautious,
   With remembrance, completely
   Pass beyond the craving of this world.

7 Those who became ordained in youth,
   Embracing what the Buddha taught,
   Illuminate the entire world
   Just as the unclouded sun and moon.

8 Those who became ordained in youth,
   Embracing what the Buddha taught,
   With remembrance, completely
   Pass beyond the craving of this world.

9 Those who, having done wrong action,
   Screen it off with their virtue,
   Are outstanding in the world
   Just like the unclouded sun and moon.

10 Those who, having done wrong actions,
    Screen it off with their virtue,
    With remembrance, completely
    Pass beyond the craving of this world.

11 Those who feel no joy for life,
    Feel no pain even at death.
    The steadfast who behold the state [of nirvana]
    Feel no sorrow though in the midst of pain.

12 Those who feel no joy for life,
    Feel no pain even at death.
    The steadfast who behold the state,
    Shine out resplendent midst their relatives.

13 Monks meditate on white [deeds],
    Eliminating black ones.

Having left home for homelessness
And developing with enjoyment
A capacity for detachment,
They give up even faint desires.

14 Conduct becomes complete in all respects
When always pure in heart,
Pure in the monk's confessional
And pure in the unsullied path.[109]

15 Just as the weeds are to the field,
The bane [of us all] is desire.
For those without desire, therefore,
A great result comes from giving.

16 Just as the weeds are to the field
The bane [of us all] is anger.
For those without anger, therefore,
A great result comes from giving.

17 Just as the weeds are to the field
The bane [of humans] is ignorance.
For those without ignorance, therefore,
A great result comes from giving.

18 Just as the weeds are to the field
The bane [of us all] is pride.
For those without pride, therefore,
A great result comes from giving.[110]

19 Just as the weeds are to the field
The bane [of humans] is attachment.
For those without attachment, therefore,
A great result comes from giving.[111]

20 Just as the weeds are to the field
The bane [of us all] is craving.
For those without craving, therefore,
A great result comes from giving.[112]

21 The sixth [the thinking mind] is owner and king.
If there is attachment, it has attachment,

And is without if there is none.[113]
[Those with] attachment are 'infants.'[114]

22 [Mind] lives within a frame of bones
Plastered over with flesh and blood.
It is a town of hate and pride,
Attachment and hypocrisy,
[A town] of misery sprung from motivation and cause:
Those who don't recognize this are ensnared in it.

23 Once realized, all rivers are quite left behind.
Non-Buddhists are not free from all those attachments.

17 *Water*

1　They [who realize this misery] do not like home;
　　With effort and remembrance,
　　Like swans leaving a stagnant pond,
　　They quit their homes and cross the river.

2　Steadfast ones who renounce the world
　　And crush all classes of demons
　　Go miraculously in space
　　Like swans on the path of the sun.

3　Those who do not have good conduct
　　And find no riches in their youth
　　Become like old worn-out seagulls
　　In dirty, turbid, fished-out ponds.

4　Those who do not have good conduct
　　And find no riches in their youth
　　Curl up like a ball and sleep,
　　Remembering the things they did before.

5　Don't think, 'The little wrongs I did
　　Will make no difference afterwards.'
　　Just as the single water drops

Fill up the vase,
So infants become filled with wrongs
Collected little by little.

6 Don't think, 'The little virtues that I did
Will make no difference afterwards.'
Just as the single water drops
Fill up the vase,
So steadfast ones are filled with virtue
Collected little by little.

7 All those that have dammed up the dirty pond,
Wanting to cross the river of the sea,
Are those who have the boats:
The navigators are the wise.[115]

8 The *Bhagavan* Buddha is [first] across.
The Brahmins are on the dry land.[116]
The monks are washing [on the other side].
The Hearers are in their boats.

9 As launderers clean with water,
And arrowsmiths straighten with fire,
As carpenters work with the wood,
The learned should subdue themselves.[117]

10 The learned ones who have great faith
Like fathomless great seas,
Free of taint and turbulence,[118]
Listen to the teachings here.

11 Thus there is water everywhere,
So who is there to run and seek [for it]?
What need for springs [to quench a thirst]?
Cut out [all] craving at its root.

12 Without attachment, like the sky,
And like a door-step unperturbed,[119]
The wise dislike this cyclic world
That is like a turbulent ocean.

18   *The Flower*

1   Who overcomes this stage [of life and death],
    The world of gods, [of humans], and of hells?
    Who are the skilful teachers of
    The four things, much desired like flowers?[120]

2   The trainees overcome this stage,
    The world of gods, [of humans], and of hells.
    They are the skilful teachers of
    The four things, much wanted like flowers.

3   Since fears arise from the forest,
    The forest, not the tree, should be cut down.
    Cutting the forests and seedlings,
    Religious persons [gain] nirvana.[121]

4   But if the seedlings are not cut,
    The subtle still makes beings take birth;[122]
    Their minds are tightly fixed by this,
    Like calves nearby their mothers wanting milk.

5   Having cut off this liking for oneself,
    Just as one plucks an autumn lotus,
    Then cultivate the path to peace
    To gain nirvana that the Buddhas teach.

6 Don't turn the words of fine teachings
   Into something that bears no fruit,
   Like pretty flowers —
   Colourful but without fragrance.

7 Conquerors travel to town [to beg],
   Just like the bees that do no harm
   To fragrances and colours of flowers,
   But sip their nectar and fly away.

8 Do not look out for others' flaws,
   For what they do or do not do,
   But look out for what one oneself
   Should do and should not do.

9 Just as fragrant and beautiful
   Pure lotus blooms arise
   From dirty rubbish heaps
   Without water,
   So too all ordinary beings who are blind
   Become transformed, out of the rubbish heap,
   Into the Hearers, and into
   Complete Buddhas with clear sight.

10 Just as many garlands are made
   From heaps of flowers,
   So every virtue big and small
   Should be done when born a human.[123]

11 Just as the *bakula* flower[124]
   Withers away in the summer,
   Monks should likewise give up hate,
   Attachment and stupidity.

12 When people have longing in their minds,
   Like accumulations of flowers,
   The Lord of Death carries them off
   Like a surging flood does a sleeping town.[125]

13 When people have longing in their minds,

Like accumulations of flowers,
The Lord of Death gains control over them
Before all their desires are satisfied.

14 When people have longing in their minds,
Like accumulations of flowers,
The Lord of Death gains control over them
Before enjoyments come about.

15 When people have longing in their minds,
Like accumulations of flowers,
The Lord of Death gains control over them
Before their work is at its end.

16 Knowing this body to be like a pot,[126]
And all phenomena like a mirage,
This great flowering of the demon is cut
Here [in this life] and death is seen no more.

17 Knowing existence[127] to be like a pot,
And all phenomena like a mirage,
This great flowering of the demon is cut
Here [in this life] and death is seen no more.

18 Knowing this body to be like foam,[128]
And all phenomena like a mirage,
The great flowering of the demon is cut
Here [in this life] and death is seen no more.

19 Knowing existence to be like foam,
And all phenomena like a mirage,
This great flowering of the demon is cut
Here [in this life] and death is seen no more.

20 Those monks who think existence essenceless,
[A thought as rare] as the *udumbara* flower,[129]
Go beyond and cast off what's not beyond[130]
Like old serpents shedding old skin.

21 Those monks who cut off all desire
Like water-flowers in ponds [cut] from the root,[131]

Go beyond and cast off what's not beyond
Like old serpents shedding old skin.

22   Those monks who cut off all hatred
Like water-flowers in ponds [cut] from the root,
Go beyond and cut off what's not beyond
Like old serpents shedding old skin.

23   Those monks who cut all ignorance
Like water-flowers in ponds [cut] from the root,
Go beyond and cast off what's not beyond
Like old serpents shedding old skin.

24   Those monks who cut all pride
Like water-flowers in ponds [cut] from the root,
Go beyond and cast off what's not beyond
Like old serpents shedding old skin.

25   Those monks who cut all attachment
Like water-flowers in ponds [cut] from the root,
Go beyond and cast off what's not beyond
Like old serpents shedding old skin.

26   Those monks who cut off all craving
Like water-flowers in ponds [cut] from the root,
Go beyond and cast off what's not beyond
Like old serpents shedding old skin.

19 The Horse

1 Just as fine horses when lashed with the whip
Are scared and gallop fast, all those with faith,
Ethics, stability and knowledge of
All things, with [subdued] powers and equipoise,
The happiness of patience, and friendship —
These [with such] protectors leave all craving behind.

2 Just as fine horses when lashed with the whip
Are scared and gallop fast, all those with faith,
Ethics, stability and knowledge of
All things, with insight and mobility[132] —
All of the protectors with remembrance
Leave every misery behind.

3 The Mighty who restrain their [sense] powers,
Just as a trainer tames a horse,
Stop anger and end contamination
And obtain even the experience of gods.

4 Like fine horses [leave] lesser nags,
The very wise give up and go
From drowsiness with vigilance
And from carelessness with caution.

5   Just as [one does not need] a whip for a fine horse,
When someone has a sense of shame,[133]
Wisdom and perfect equipoise
Wrongdoing is removed.

6   One takes the tamed [horse] to the field
    [of games or war]
And on the tamed [horse] rides forth the king.
Those who are patient when abused,
The tamed, are best among all humans.

7   Taming oneself is better than
Taming a highstrung thoroughbred,
Taming the mightiest of elephants
Better than breaking mules.
[Those] skilful ones who properly
Subdue themselves find peace;
All of these other mounts
Can never actually achieve that state.

8   Taming oneself is better than
Taming a highstrung thoroughbred,
Taming the mightiest of elephants
Better than breaking mules.
Those with remembrance who properly
Subdue themselves go to the end of pain;
All of these other mounts
Can never actually achieve that state.

9   Taming oneself is better than
Taming a highstrung thoroughbred,
Taming the mightiest of elephants
Better than breaking mules.
Those with remembrance who properly
Subdue themselves give up [bad] migrations;
All of these other mounts
Can never actually achieve that state.

10   Taming oneself is better than
Taming a highstrung thoroughbred,

Taming the mightiest of elephants
Better than breaking mules,
For those who properly subdue themselves
Sever and leave clasping behind;
All of these other mounts
Can never actually achieve that state.[134]

11   Just as a trainer tames a fine horse
Similarly one should tame oneself.
By properly taming oneself,
The limits of all pain are passed.

12   Since one's own lord[135] is just oneself
And oneself is one's own refuge,
Just as a trainer tames a fine horse
Similarly one should subdue oneself.

20 *Wrath*

1 When wrath and all conceit are given up,
   All clasps[136] are left behind, and attachment
   For name and form no more, then there is nothing
   At all for which attachments can arise.

2 Give up wrath the moment it occurs,
   And attachments [just] when they arise.[137]
   The steadfast expel ignorance,
   And seeing truth find happiness.

3 One sleeps in peace when wrath is given up;
   One is not tormented by pain.

4 Monks, destroy [as well as] wrath,
   The root poison that destroys happiness.
   By doing so one ends sorrow
   And earns praise from Superiors.

5 Whoever becomes enraged and shouts,
   'I did it well! There's nothing wrong!'
   Is tormented when the wrath subsides,
   As though by burning flames.

6 Without regret or embarrassment
   The wrathful lack all shame.[138]
   Nobody relies on a person
   Completely overcome with rage.

7 The power of strong infantile beings
   Is no power at all.
   The infantile without religion
   Have no hope of accomplishment.

8 Those who are powerful, but still
   Show tolerance toward the poor,
   Their patience, it's said, is best —
   They always care for and respect the weak.

9 Those who, though in authority
   Show tolerance toward the poor,
   Their patience, it's said, is best —
   They always care for and respect the weak.

10 The strong who are patient
    Even in the face of gross provocation,
    Their patience, it's said, is best —
    They always care for and respect the weak.[139]

11 The strong who are patient
    Even in the face of gross abuse,
    Their patience, it's said, is best —
    They always care for and respect the weak.

12 Those who remain tranquil
    When they perceive another's wrath,
    Protect themselves and other beings
    From every great anxiety.

13 Those who remain tranquil
    When they perceive another's wrath,
    Do work that has advantage for
    Both themselves and for other beings.

14 All beings unskilled in religion

Think easily, 'They are infants'
Of those who do this work which has
Advantage for themselves and others.

15   But holy beings emphasize that the patience
Of those who tolerate inferiors' words
Excels the patience of one fearing a master's words,
And the patience toward an equal's taunt to fight.

16   Infantile beings think they have won
When they hurl abuse in wrath.
The person who tolerates those words
Is always victorious.

17   Don't be wrathful; say what is true;
Make charity, however small,
To those who beg:[140] these three provide
Foundation for celestial births.

18   Those besides themselves with rage
Don't even see their own purpose.
Take care in cyclic existence —
Refrain from speaking words of wrath.

19   Since those who answer wrath with wrath
Turn into wicked beings,
Those answering wrath with wrathlessness
Win the hard battle, valiantly.

20   Wrathlessness can withstand wrath
And good withstand what is not good.
Benevolence can withstand avarice
And truth withstand what is not true.

21   How could a calm person, with right livelihood
And without wrath become wrathful?
Freed by their knowledge of the truth
The wise are without wrath.

22   Though Superiors always devote themselves
To remaining without wrath and cruelty,

All wrathful, wicked beings
Tower like intractable mountains.

23   Those who control their wrath when it rears up
As they would a horse when it strays loose,
I call 'the best trainers'; those who
[Must] rope it down are common beings.[141]

21 *The One Gone Thus*

1   Who could teach me, all-knowing of this world,
    Outshining all, untainted here by anything,
    Completely free, without craving, released,
    Who alone has achieved omniscience?

2   Who could teach me, unequalled and unique,
    Who found enlightenment and who alone can teach it,
    I, the One Gone Thus, all-powerful
    And omniscient teacher of humans and gods?

3   I am this world's Foe Destroyer,
    Matchless throughout the universe.
    I am the king throughout celestial realms,
    For I have overcome all demons.

4   Since there is no one who is like me
    I have no one for a master.
    I alone found matchless, complete
    Enlightenment here in this world.[142]

5   Know those like me who found the end
    Of contamination to be the kings.[143]
    I conquered what is wrong
    And thereby conquered afflictions.

6 Since worldly people could not know
   The origin [of buddhahood] unless they are taught,
   I went to Varanasi,
   An all-knowing Buddha in nirvana,
   Beyond all craving for the world,
   And beating the drum of the teaching
   Turned the wheel of the dharma[144]
   Which no one in this world had turned.

7 Heroic Ones Gone Thus
   Subdue this world with their teaching.
   No scholar would disdain the way
   They pacify with their teaching.

8 The gods and humans take pleasure
   In beings of quick intelligence
   Who have taken final bodies —
   Those reckoned as the perfect Buddhas
   Who sit steadfast in *samādhi*,
   Renounced of the world, and abiding in peace.

9 The nature of the completed Buddhas —
   All Buddhas of the past,
   And all Buddhas yet to come,
   And all those now in perfect buddhahood,
   Those who have worked before,
   Will work, or who are working now
   To eliminate the many sorrows —
   Is to revere the holy religion.

10 So if you like [to help] yourself,
    And want eminence in this world,
    Have recollection of Buddha's teaching
    And revere the holy doctrine.

11 All those infants who have no faith
    In what the Buddha taught
    Proceed into the place of sorrow
    Like the merchants lured by cannibals.[145]

12 All the wise ones who generate
    Faith in the teaching of Buddha
    Proceed across to happiness
    Like the merchants who had the horse.

13 Ones Gone Thus, unequalled and unique
    Buddhas, who work with both conceptions
    Of happiness and likewise detachment,[146]
    Dispel dullness, go beyond, and have renown.

14 They found the prize, have power over mind,
    Are free, uncontaminated, quite free,
    Free at heart without strife and contamination,[147]
    Looking to help worldly beings.

15 Like people on a mountain peak
    Look down on all below,
    So too, those pure-hearted and free from pain
    Who reach the height of the dharma abode,
    Look down on all those suffering
    With the burdensome pain of birth and death,
    And open the door to immortality.
    You who want to hear, remove all doubt.

22 *Listening*

1 Fine the listening and fine the deeds,
   Fine the getting out of home,
   Fine what encircles the eliminator
   And that compatible with religious practice.[148]

2 Unwise and infantile beings
   Act as though they are immortal.
   The wise, like sick people at night,
   Work at the holy religion.

3 Just as those living in the gloom
   Of a heavily-curtained home
   Don't see the objects which are there
   Even though they have the eyes to see,
   So too, those with intelligence,
   Though of [noble] lineage in this human [world],
   Don't understand, until they hear
   The dharma of wrongs and virtue.
   Just as those who have eyes can see
   All of the objects with a lamp,
   So too, understanding occurs [from]
   Hearing the dharma of wrongs and virtue.

4   By listening, all religions
    Are understood, wrongs are removed.
    By listening, what is meaningless
    Is given up and nirvana is attained.

5   Though one has listened many times,
    Yet if not governed by good ethics
    One's ethics are a cause for scorn:
    That listening is not complete.

6   Though one has not listened many times,
    Yet if governed by good ethics,
    One's ethics are a cause for praise:
    That listening becomes complete.

7   If one has not listened many times
    And is not governed by good ethics,
    From both sides there is cause for scorn:
    There is not complete probity.

8   If one has listened many times
    And is governed by good ethics
    From both sides there is cause for praise
    There is complete probity.[149]

9   Like this earth's golden ornaments,
    No one at all disparages
    Those with much listening, who hold
    Religion, are wise and in equipoise.

10 All those inferring [me] from form,
    Evaluating me from voice,
    Those beings who have longing desire,
    Have no understanding of me.[150]

11 If there is inner understanding
    And the external is not seen,
    This inner result is a seeing
    Which words can lead astray.[151]

12 If the external is seen

And there is no inner understanding,
This outer result is a seeing
Which words can lead astray.

13 If there's neither inner understanding
Nor is the external seen,
The infant is completely obscured
And words can lead [that one] astray.

14 If there is inner understanding
And the external is seen,
The wise, renounced, exemplary one
Cannot be led astray by words.

15 Though most everything has been heard
And many things been seen,
The steadfast don't properly base
Their trust on what they heard and saw.

16 Though the essence is known [from] listening
To fine words, and known [from] all *samādhi*,
Understanding and listening have no
Great benefit to careless profligates.

17 Whoever likes the doctrine that Superiors teach,
Whose conduct of body and speech accords with that,
They're patient, befriended by joy, and restrained,[152]
And achieve hearing, and wisdom's farther shore.

23 *Self*

1   Put into practice the fine words.
     Support and serve religious persons.
     Retreat in detachment
     And pacify your mind.[153]

2   In retreat with one place to sleep,
     Avoiding every laziness,
     Live in the forest all alone
     And all alone subdue yourself.

3   Whoever triumphs over self
     Achieves a conquest greater than
     The conquerors who win
     A hundred thousand victories in war.

4   Those who, by always keeping vows,
     Become subdued and conquer self,
     Their triumph is supreme;
     Other conquests are just common.

5   Neither the demon nor Brahmā
     Nor any god or spirit can vanquish self.
     Abiding with intelligence
     Only the monk triumphs over that.

6 After grounding yourself properly
   Then tame all others as you did yourself.
   If one first grounds oneself properly
   When taming [others] one is skilled and unafflicted.

7 Just as you first did for yourself[154]
   Likewise do the same for others too.
   Being tamed and peaceful oneself,
   One effortlessly tames others.

8 Just as you first did for yourself
   Likewise do the same for others too.
   Take heed! tame oneself well.
   When one is tamed, one becomes skilled.

9 For your own needs first set aside
   The many needs of everybody else;
   If one's need is seen to be great,
   One's need becomes most excellent.[155]

10 I am the master of myself
    Who else can be my master?
    The master of myself, I'm skilled,
    And will attain every purpose.

11 I am the master of myself
    Who else can be my master?
    The master of myself, I'm skilled,
    And will attain all religion.

12 I am the master of myself
    Who else can be my master?
    The master of myself, I'm skilled
    And will become a famous person.[156]

13 I am the master of myself
    Who else can be my master?
    The master of myself, I'm skilled
    And will achieve great happiness.

14 I am the master of myself
    Who else can be my master?

The master of myself, I'm skilled
And will gain birth in happy realms.[157]

15   I am the master of myself
Who else can be my master?
The master of myself, I'll attain
The lasting happiness of heaven.

16   I am the master of myself
Who else can be my master?
The master of myself, I stand out
Eminent amongst my friends.

17   I am the master of myself
Who else can be my master?
The master of myself, in the midst
Of pain there is no suffering.

18   I am the master of myself
Who else can be my master?
The master of myself, I cut off
All [attachments'] bonds.[158]

19   I am the master of myself
Who else can be my master?
The master of myself, I give up
Birth in every bad migration.[159]

20   I am the master of myself
Who else can be my master?
The master of myself, I gain
Liberation from all sorrow.[160]

21   I am the master of myself
Who else can be my master?
The master of myself, I will
Attain mastery of myself.[161]

22   I am the master of myself
Who else can be my master?
The master of myself, I'm close
To actual nirvana.[162]

24 Comparisons

1 It is better to listen to
One line with the meaning of peace,
Than to recite a hundred lines
Of meaningless verse.[163]

2 It is better to listen to
One line about the truth of peace,
Than to recite a hundred lines
Of truthless verse.

3 It is better to live a day or two
Ethically, with equipoise,
Than live one hundred years
In licentious agitation.

4 It is better to live a day or two
In steady perseverence,
Than live one hundred years
In slothful inactivity.

5 It is better to live a day or two
With equipoise and great wisdom,
Than live one hundred years
In foolish agitation.

6 It is better to live a day or two
Seeing arising and perishing,[164]
Than live one hundred years
Without that sight.

7 It is better to live a day or two
Seeing feelings' end,[165]
Than live one hundred years
Without that sight.

8 It is better to live a day or two
Seeing contaminations' end,[166]
Than live one hundred years
Without that sight.

9 It is better to live a day or two
Seeing the immutable state,[167]
Than live one hundred years
Without that sight.

10 It is better to live a day or two
Discerning that state so hard to see,[168]
Than live one hundred years
Without that sight.

11 It is better to live a day or two
Discerning that exalted state,
Than live one hundred years
Without that sight.

12 It is better to live a day or two
Discerning the holy state,[169]
Than live one hundred years
Without that sight.

13 It is better to live a day or two
Discerning the immortal state,[170]
Than live one hundred years
Without that sight.

14 It is better to live a day or two

Discerning the nectarous state,[171]
Than live one hundred years
Without that sight.

15 It is better to live a day or two
Discerning the dustless state,[172]
Than live one hundred years
Without that sight.

16 It is better to live a day or two
Discerning the dust-free state,[173]
Than live one hundred years
Without that sight.

17 An offering for just a little time
To one meditating on self
Is far better
Than a century of fire offerings —
A hundred years devoted to
One's jungle sacrificial fire.

18 Only eating food with the tip
Of kusha grass each month,
Can't match even a sixteenth part
Of faith in the Enlightened One.[174]

19 Only eating food with the tip
Of kusha grass each month,
Can't match even a sixteenth part
Of faith in the holy Doctrine.

20 Only eating food with the tip
Of kusha grass each month,
Can't match even a sixteenth part
Of faith in the Community.

21 Only eating food with the tip
Of kusha grass each month,
Can't match even a sixteenth part
Of compassion for all sentient beings.

22 Only eating food with the tip
    Of kusha grass each month,
    Can't match even a single part
    Of compassion for all living beings.

23 Only eating food with the tip
    Of kusha grass each month,
    Can't match even a sixteenth part
    Of compassion for the malevolent.

24 Only eating food with the tip
    Of kusha grass each month,
    Can't match even a sixteenth part
    Of harbouring kind thoughts.

25 Only eating food with the tip
    Of kusha grass each month,
    Can't match even a sixteenth part
    Of the holy dharma of fine words.[175]

26 Making a century of
    A thousand offerings each month,
    Can't match even a sixteenth part
    Of faith in the Enlightened One.

27 Making a century of
    A thousand offerings each month,
    Can't match even a sixteenth part
    Of faith in the holy Doctrine.

28 Making a century of
    A thousand offerings each month,
    Can't match even a sixteenth part
    Of faith in the Community.

29 Making a century of
    A thousand offerings each month,
    Can't match even a sixteenth part
    Of compassion for all sentient beings.

30 Making a century of

A thousand offerings each month,
Can't match even a sixteenth part
Of compassion for all living beings.

31 Making a century of
A thousand offerings each month,
Can't match even a sixteenth part
Of compassion for the malevolent.

32 Making a century of
A thousand offerings each month,
Can't match even a sixteenth part
Of harbouring kind thoughts.

33 Making a century of
A thousand offerings each month,
Can't match even a sixteenth part
Of the holy dharma of fine words.

34 Any burnt offerings and gifts to worldly [beings]
Made by a person who wants merits
Cannot match even one quarter
Of a prostration made with sincere thought.

Folio Three

25 *Intimate Friends*

1 Wise ones, do not befriend
The faithless, who are mean
And slanderous and cause schism.
Don't take bad people as your companions.

2 Wise ones, be intimate
With the faithful who speak gently,[176]
Are ethical and do much listening.
Take the best as companions.

3 Do not devote yourself
To bad companions and wicked beings.
Devote yourself to holy people,
And to spiritual friends.

4 By devotion to people like that
You will do goodness, not wrong.

5 By devotion to faithful and wise people
Who have heard much and pondered many things,[177]
By heeding their fine words, even from afar,
Their special qualities are attained here.

6 Since those devoted to inferiors degenerate,

Those to equals mark time,
And those to great ones attain sanctity,
Be devoted to those great ones.

7 By devotion to ethical,
Calm, and most knowledgeable great beings,
One attains to a greatness
Greater even than the great.

8 Just as the clean kusha grass
That wraps a rotten fish
Will also start to rot,
So too will those devoted to an evil person.

9 Just as a leaf folded
To contain an incense offering
Also becomes sweet,
So too will those devoted to the virtuous.

10 When one does no wrong yet
Is devoted to evil people,
One will still be abused,
For others suppose that this one too is bad.

11 The devotee acquires the same faults
As the person not worthy of devotion,
Like an untainted arrow smeared
With the poison of a tainted sheath.

12 Steadfast ones who fear the taint of faults,
Do not befriend bad people.
By close reliance and devotion
To one's companion,
Soon one becomes just like
The object of one's devotion.

13 Therefore, knowing that one's devotion
Is like the casing of the fruit,[178]
The wise devote themselves to holy,
Not to unholy people,
And drawn along the monk's path
They find the end of misery.

14 Just as a spoon cannot taste the sauce,[179]
    Infantile ones do not understand
    The doctrine, even after
    A lifetime of devotion to the wise.

15 Just as the tongue can taste the sauce.
    Those with wisdom can understand
    The entire doctrine, after just
    A brief attendance on the wise.

16 Because infantile ones lack eyes to see,
    Though they devote their lifetimes
    To the wise, they never
    Understand the entire doctrine.
    Those with wisdom fully understand
    The entire doctrine after just
    A brief attendance on the wise.
    They have eyes to see.

17 Though they devote their lifetimes
    To wise beings, infantile ones
    Do not understand the doctrine
    Of the Buddha in its entirety.
    Those with wisdom understand
    The doctrine of the Buddha
    In its entirety after just
    A brief attendance on the wise.

18 Even just one meaningful line
    Sets the wise ones to their task,
    But all the teaching that the Buddhas gave
    Won't set infantile ones to work.

19 The intelligent will understand
    A hundred lines from one,
    But for the infantile beings
    A thousand lines do not suffice for one.[180]

20 [If one must chose between them],
    Better the wise even if unfriendly.
    No infant is suited to be a friend.

Sentient beings intimate with
The infant-like are led to hell.

21   Wise persons are those who know
Infantile ones for what they are:
'Infantile ones' are those
Who take infants to be the wise.

22   The censure of the wise
Is far preferable
To the eulogy or praise
Of the infant.

23   Devotion to infants brings misery.
Since they are like one's foe,
It is best to never see or hear
Or have devotion for such people.

24   Like meeting friends, devotion to
The steadfast causes happiness.

25   Therefore, like the revolving stars and moon,
Devote yourself to the steadfast, moral ones
Who have heard much, who draw on what is best —
The kind, the pure, the best superior ones.

26 *Nirvana*

1 The monk contracts conceptual thought,
   Like the tortoise his limbs into his shell,
   Not relying, nor doing others harm —
   In nirvana, not scorned by anyone.[181]

2 Patience, the Buddha says, is the best austerity,
   And the best patience is nirvana.[182]

3 Ordained people who harm others
   Are certainly not religious people.

4 Do not speak even one harsh word.
   Once spoken there will be response.
   From words which sow discord,
   Come misery and later punishments.

5 If I retaliate
   It is like striking on a gong.
   The experience of life and death
   In cyclic existence goes on and on.

6 If I do not retaliate
   It's like not striking on a gong.

Then discord does not pile up
And nirvana is thus attained.

7   Freedom from sickness is a holy gift;
Contentment is opulence.
[Indulgence] the finest friend,
And nirvana the finest bliss.

8   Pervading misery is odious,
Of all sickness, hunger unbearable.[183]
To the extent that this is known
Nirvana becomes the best.

9   Few go to happy migrations,
Uncountable numbers to bad.
When the fault is realized
Nirvana is quickly attained.

10   Happy migration has its cause,
And bad migration has its cause.
Going to nirvana is caused,
So there are causes for them all.

11   Fine woods are the animals' range,
The sky the range of all the birds;
The dharma is the range of intellect,
Nirvana is the Foe Destroyers' range.[184]

12   A feeble effort and small mind
And lack of understanding in this [task]
Will not procure the liberation
Where every knot has been severed.

13   Just as the rowboat is lightened
When you bail all the water out,
So too nirvana is attained
When hate and greed are given up.

14   That which arose before does not [now] arise,
That which has not arisen arises.
[In nirvana there is no affliction] that arose or will arise
Or which arises at present.[185]

15 Understanding the hard to see, the limitless,
A happiness unseen, [having become a] knower of truth,
And seeing no craving and liking:
The end of misery is, then, like this.[186]

16 All craving is severed,
Attachment really given up,
From the lake now dry there is no flow:[187]
The end of misery is, then, like this.

17 The body destroyed, feelings cooled down,[188]
Discrimination stopped, volition
At peace, and consciousness subdued:
The end of misery is, then, like this.

18 When looking becomes just seeing,
When listening becomes just hearing,
When realizing just realization,
When being conscious just consciousness:
The end of misery is, then, like this.[189]

19 This, mother, pain and great pain:
The end of misery is, then, like this.[190]

20 No hope, no loves, in complete peace,
Free from attachment always:
The end of misery is, then, like this.[191]

Where the basis exists, deeds come about.[192] Where deeds
exist, straying comes about. Where straying exists, inflexibility comes about. Where inflexibility exists, going and
coming come about. Where going and coming exist, transmigration at death comes about. Where transmigration has
taken place in this way, birth, old age, sickness and death,
sorrow, cries of anguish, miseries, mental unhappiness and
strife[193] arise. This which is simply a great heap of misery
arises.

Where the basis does not exist, deeds do not come about.[194]
Where deeds no not exist, straying does not come about.
Where straying has not come about, flexibility comes into

being. Where there is flexibility, going and coming do not come about. Where going and coming do not exist, transmigration does not come about. Where transmigration does not exist, birth, old age, sickness and death, sorrow, cries of anguish, miseries, mental unhappiness and strife are all stopped. This which is simply a great heap of misery is stopped.

O monks! the unborn, unoriginated, unfabricated, uncompounded, unarising exists. Birth, origination, fabrication, mental production, composition, and interdependent arising exist.

O monks! were the unborn, unoriginated, unfabricated, uncompounded, unarising not to exist, I would not state that there is the definite emergence from birth, origination, fabrication, mental production, composition, and interdependent arising.

O monks! it is because the unborn, unoriginated, unfabricated, uncompounded, unarising exists that I state there is the definite emergence from birth, origination, fabrication, composition, mental production and interdependent arising.

21 Don't like what will perish, what is
    Born, arisen, and originated,
    Is fabricated, composite and unstable
    And arises from the stream of food.

22 Happiness is peace on the basis
    Of renunciation and rough and subtle
    Investigation, [when] every misery
    Is stopped and composites[195] are at peace.

O monks! with clairvoyance I see [it] does not abide anywhere. For it does not abide in the earth, the water, the fire or the wind. It does not abide in the source[196] of boundless space, in the source of boundless consciousness, in the source of nothingness, or in the source of neither existence nor non-existence of discrimination. And it does not abide in this world or the next, on the moon or on the sun. There is no observation of it.

O monks! I do not state that going and coming exist there, for there is no abiding. I do not state that there is transmigration for there is no arising. The end of misery is, then, like this.

23 It does not abide anywhere:
    In earth, in water, fire or wind.
    There whiteness does not illuminate
    Nor does darkness exist there.
    There the moon does not appear.
    There the sun does not shine out.

24 It is the knowledge of those
    Who are Brahmin Conquerors.[197]
    It is freedom from formlessness,
    From forms and every misery.

25 [Nirvana is] the destination, [is] fearlessness,
    [Is] without regrets and vanity.
    The pains of life are chopped to bits,
    So the last body is reached.

26 The ultimate destination —
    This is a state of peace without equal
    Where all signification ends —
    A pure freedom which is immortal.

27 Emerging from what is and what is not
    Comparable, Buddhas give up the composite,[198]
    With inner joy and equipoise
    They crack open the shell and emerge.

28 The gift of teaching surpasses all gifts,
    The happiness of [hearing] teaching, all happiness,
    The power of patience surpasses all power,
    The end of craving surpasses all bliss.

27 *Seeing*

1 Like chaff that is tossed up,
   Somebody else's faults
   Are seen more easily than one's own.
   One's own faults are hard to see.[199]

2 The person always finding fault
   Is like a cheater playing dice
   Hiding the truth about himself
   And looking out for others' faults.
   Dharma recedes far from sight —
   It makes the crooked dharma thrive.

3 Chattering, and stealing unabashed,
   Raven-like, with filthy actions,
   Those whose habits are most afflicted
   Live an easy shameless life.[201]

4 Always seeking for cleanliness,
   Not being coarse, exercising restraint,
   Pure in livelihood and beliefs:
   Life with a sense of shame is hard.

5 These worldly beings are blind.

Those with insight are few.
As [few] birds escape from a snare
Hardly any enjoy high birth.

6 Infants ensnared by their bodies
Revolve through a cycle of darkness.[202]
Worldly beings attached to wealth
Look, as it were, on other stuff.[203]

7 Thinking 'I brought these people forth'
And 'That other being has done it'
They see as truth what is not true
And therefore do not see at all.[204]

8 Hardly any see this [selflessness],
They do not see the sharp pain.[205]

9 Beings who crave objects[206] have attachment.
Those who have already seen that sharp pain
Hold neither the view 'I have done it,'
Nor, 'It was done by someone else.'

10 All the living beings have pride,
Are attached and fettered by pride.
These disputatious people
Do not reverse the wheel [of life].[207]

11 All that has been achieved
And all that is to be achieved
Are both covered over by dust.[208]
After [understanding this, Superiors] train as sick
persons.

Those who make an essence[209] and are at one extreme, are
those who are ethical and train themselves, have good
conduct, pure behaviour, undertake austerities and attend on
protectors, etc.

Those holding such a belief in self say, 'Desire [for sex] is
clean, desire is meritorious, desire is to be enjoyed, desire is
without fault'; all who take [as path to liberation] the conduct

which falls into what is intensely desired are also at an extreme.

All those two extremes [of action] make bigger the [living] graveyards. For by those actions the graveyards have become bigger. Some of those who do not see these two extremes are lustful, [believe enjoyment from desires to be virtue]. Others chase after things, [exhaust themselves in meaningless practices]. Those who [realize the two extremes for what they are] see those people to be lustful and chasing after things.

Those who do see these two extremes are not lustful and do not chase after things. Those who have eyes also see that these people do not have intense lust and do not chase after things intensely. Those who see selflessness do not act like that [take enjoyment of desire as path]. They do not think like that. They do not designate [a course of action followed by a person substantially different to aggregates] to be the path. The end of misery is like this.[210]

12 Those who look at this transient world
    Just as one looks at a bubble,
    And as one looks at a mirage,
    Are not seen by the King of Death.

13 Those who look upon the body[211]
    Just as one looks at a bubble,
    And as one looks at a mirage,
    Are not seen by the King of Death.

14 The wise do not become attached
    To what attracts infantile beings.
    Look on this body always
    As a colourful royal chariot.[212]

15 The wise do not become confused
    By what confuses infantile beings.
    Look on this body always,
    As a colourful royal chariot.

16 Through this [attachment to body] infants degenerate,
   Like old elephants stuck in mud.
   Look on this body always
   As a colourful royal chariot.

17 Always look upon this body
   Which does not abide unchangingly
   As a diseased and transient thing
   Similar to a wound one has received.

18 Look on this body all adorned
   With rubies, earrings and bracelets
   As a diseased and transient thing
   Which does not abide continuously.

19 Hair-styles ornamented with braids,
   And eyes made up with eye-shadow
   Confuse the infant-like beings,
   But not those working for the other side.

20 Eyes freshly painted with make-up,
   Ornamented bodies of pus
   Confuse the infant-like beings,
   But not those working for the other side.

21 The body, fragrant with perfume,
   With legs bedaubed with red colour
   Confuses infant-like beings,
   But not those working for the other side.

22 Those who, clasped to desire, have attachment
   And do not see the fault in clasping,
   Who are attached to having what they desire
   Do not cross the vast endless river.

23 The best, final, and fully unattached ones
   Do not view self or mine in this [world],[213]
   And thus freed, they cross over the river
   Not crossed before, and are not reborn again.

24 Come here! Have a look at this person

In freedom bonds, who left the thicket
And thicketless gave up the woods
And ran away to the forest.214

25 Behold the travel, without wickedness
In carriages spread with white canopies,
With matching spokes, and pleasing parts.215
Cut the continuum of chains.

26 Most of those petrified with fright
Go for refuge to the woods,216
To gardens, and to sacred groves,
To temples and to trees.

27 Those are not the foremost refuge.
Those are not the finest refuge.
By taking refuge in those things
One is not freed from all misery.

28 When those who've gone for refuge to
The Buddha, Doctrine and Community217
Are travelling to nirvana,
It is the eightfold path
Of Superiors that sees with wisdom
All four truths of Superior beings:
The misery, its origin,
Complete passing from misery,
And happiness [the path].
That is the finest refuge,
That is the holy refuge.
By taking refuge in that place
One is freed from all misery.218

29 See by seeing; with sight, see the unseen.219
[Those who] see with nonsight don't see what
    should be seen.
Simulated sight is said to be separate from insight,
Just as day and night don't meet in one place.

30 There is no seeing from simulated sight;

If there is seeing, it isn't simulated —
This seeing is not affected:
One with affected sight doesn't see.

31   One with affected sight doesn't see anything;
If one sees what [it is], seeing isn't simulated.
One who sees like that is separate from
The one with simulated sight.

32   When one does not see suffering
Then one sees 'self';
To the extent that suffering is perceived,
Seeing is not affected.

33   If [seeing] the arising of events is obscured by
        anything,
Then composites are not seen as suffering.
Therefore, if [obscured], seeing is simulated;
If without [obscuration], it is not.

28 *Evil*

1 Here is the teaching of Buddha:
Do not do any evil deed.
Completely perfect all virtue.
Completely pacify your mind.

2 Merit increases greatly from giving.
The well-controlled don't collect enemies.
Virtue eliminates evil.
Nirvana is the end of affliction.[220]

3 Better live with the wise or even alone,
Than with the infantile and those alloyed.[221]
Those who are wise abandon evil beings
Like swans which extract milk from water.

4 Superiors who see the flaw
Of this world and see the cessation of it
Do not take pleasure in evil.
The evil do not like virtue.

5 Tasting the excellent flavour
Of peace and complete detachment,
Plagues and evil are no more:
The taste of liking dharma is imbibed.[222]

6   When mental contamination
    Is gone and chains don't warp the mind,
    When virtue and evil are left behind,
    All bad migrations hold no fear.[223]

7   Rely on people who turn one from
    Unfounded ways and speak of good,
    Who show the consequence, and are
    Scholars, confuting [falsity] and speaking [truth].
    If one relies on such people
    Good not evil comes about.

8   Liberated and in great peace,
    Speaking gently without conceit,
    They shake out every evil deed
    Like wind shaking the leaves from trees.[224]

9   Like dust that's thrown into the wind,
    Pure ones who have no afflictions,
    Nor wrath, stop the evil response
    To the infants who become angry with them.

10 To the doer of virtue, virtue;
    To the doer of evil, evil.
    All deeds that someone has done
    Will each be met by that very same person.

11 The afflictive response is mine alone
    If I have done an evil deed,
    And mine alone the purity
    If I did not do evil.

12 No one does another's work,
    Pure or impure, [the person alone] does the work.

13 The evil I myself have done,
    And accumulated quickly,
    Ruins and overcomes my mind
    Like diamonds boring into gems.

14 Just as pedestrians with [open] eyes
    Proceed along a frightful path,

The wise here in this world
Abandon every evil deed.

15   The wise abandon evil beings
Like the wealthy a glut of friends,
Like merchant traders fearful roads,
Like those who want to live, poison.

16   Just as poison has no effect
Even when taken in the palm
Which has no open wound, so too
There is no evil unless the deed was done.

17   To do wrong and what is without
Benefit to oneself is easy.
That most excellent work which brings
Pleasure and benefits is hard.

18   That evil which is easy for bad persons
Superiors find hard to do.
The holy find goodness easy,
And evil most difficult to do.

19   Pleasures delight the infants' minds
Until fruition of evil.
Their minds are filled with torment
When fruition of evil occurs.[225]

20   Until fruition of evil
They view the evil deed as fine.
They look on it as evil
When fruition of evil occurs.

21   Until fruition of goodness
They view the goodness as evil.
They look on it as goodness
When fruition of goodness occurs.

22   Since it amasses misery
Don't take pleasure in evil deeds.
Though done once in a hundred times
Don't do them time and time again.

23   Since it amasses happiness,
     Take pleasure in making merit.
     Even if merit has been made
     Keep doing so time and time again.

24   Instead of loving evil deeds
     And leisurely making merit,
     Make haste to make merit and turn
     The mind away from wickedness.

25   Even a tiny evil deed
     Can cause great ruin and trouble
     In the world that lies beyond —
     Like poison that has entered the body.

26   Even small meritorious acts
     Bring happiness to future lives,
     Accomplishing a great purpose
     Like seeds becoming bounteous crops.

27   The one who becomes enraged at those
     Without anger, and [who] hurts the innocent,
     Will quickly achieve [in return]
     Simply one of ten endowments:
     Unbearable experience,[226]
     Or physical dismemberment,
     Or else excruciating pain,
     Or becoming mentally disturbed,
     Or wrenched away from kin and friends,
     Or running out of all enjoyments,
     Or facing the cruelty of the king,
     Or hearing unbearable abuse,
     Or else a great conflagration
     Will certainly burn down that person's home,
     Or tenth, that person obtains a bad rebirth
     After death as a simpleton.

28   When evil has been done there is no ease.
     There is no ease even though it was done
     In solitude, long past or far away.
     There is fruition, so there is no ease.

29   When merits have been made, then there is ease.
     There is an experience of ease, though they were made
     In solitude, long past or far away.
     There is fruition, therefore there is ease.

30   The evil I have done causes anguish,
     Causes torment even though it was done
     In solitude, long past or far away.
     There is fruition which causes anguish.
     Seeing that I myself possess black deeds
     Causes anguish here and elsewhere as well.
     The evil done causes twofold anguish —
     Anguish that is intense torment.[227]

31   The merits I have made bring happiness,
     Bring gladness even though they were made
     In solitude, long past or far away.
     There is fruition which brings happiness.
     Seeing that I myself possess pure deeds[228]
     Brings happiness here and elsewhere as well.
     The merit made brings twofold happiness —
     Happiness that is intense gladness.

32   The evil I have done causes sorrow,
     Causes grief even though it was done
     In solitude, long past or far away.
     There is fruition which causes sorrow.
     Seeing that I myself possess black deeds
     Causes sorrow here and in the beyond.
     The evil done causes twofold sorrow —
     Sorrow that is intense grief.

33   The merits I have made bring happiness,
     Bring delight even though they were made
     In solitude, long past or far away.
     There is fruition which brings happiness.
     Seeing that I myself possess white deeds[229]
     Brings happiness here and in the beyond.
     The merits made bring twofold happiness —
     Happiness that is intense delight.

34   Like rotten ships sinking into the sea,
     Death brings terror to those with evil deeds —
     Irreligious persons who spurned dharma,
     Who have done evil and have made no merit.[230]

35   Like a strong ship reaching the farther shore,
     Death never brings terror to me
     Who has made merit and done no evil,
     And has done the dharma[231] taught by the holy ones.

29 *Antitheses*

1 Just as the fireflies appear
Until the sun begins to shine,
And when the sun is shining
Turn dowdy and do not appear,
So too philosophers appear
Until the Ones Gone Thus start to shine
And when the Universal Buddha shines
Those [philosophers] with their listeners do not
show up.[232]

2 Liking what is not likeable
Not liking what is likeable[233]
Those whose conduct is misconceived[234]
Do not attain the likeable.

3 Discerning in the true light
What is likeable and what is not,
Those whose conduct is well conceived
Attain that which is likeable.

4 [Those who are] clinging to their beliefs, and to what
they've heard,

Making anew and increasing their bonds:
They race and live within this cyclic world
Like moths flying into the flames.[235]

5 By striving, good work, and cogitation,
Completely give up all that is
Experienced here or in another [life],
And all one's present various doubts.[236]

6 Those who wear the saffron robes
[While] in a state of degeneracy,
Have no right to put them on
Since they lack calmness and resolve.

7 Those who've given up degeneracy
And have fine ethics and equipoise,
Are fit to put on saffron robes
Since they have calmness and resolve.

8 Mere good colour or good build,
Or a mere way with words,
Does not place in the first rank[237]
Those who are crafty, false and miserly.

9 Whoever has severed those three,
Like cutting the top of a palmyra,[238]
And who is wise and free of fault
Is said to be in the first rank.

10 Most people in this world who aren't controlled
Deceive [others] with signs of good control.
Check well before you trust someone: don't trust
From seeing build or colour once or twice.

11 Those noble outside but bad within,
Like brass that is not what it seems,
Or iron-alloy gilded with gold,
Roam this world with their retinue.

12 People who bloat themselves and fall asleep
And spend all night and day in sloth,

Like fat hogs wallowing in mud,
Time and again enter a lowly womb.

13   Humans who always are mindful
And know the right amount to eat
Find less misery, and their slow
Digestion also gives longer life.

14   The lazy and forgetful people
Who do not control their senses
And know the right amount to eat,
View and deal with [the body] as if clean.
They are destroyed by attachment,
Like unstable trees by wind.

15   Those who strive hard and are mindful
And know the right amount to eat,
Who keep their senses under control
And view and deal with [the body] as unclean
Are not ruffled by attachment,
Like unmoving mountains and the wind.

16   People don't like hermitages[239]
Although they should really be enjoyed.
Those free from desires enjoy them;
Those chasing after desires do not.

17   Wheresoever Superiors live,
In towns or in a hermitage,
In deep valleys or on the plains,
That place is ever beautiful.

18   Holy beings are seen from afar
Like a range of snow mountains;
Cruel persons, like arrows shot in gloom,
Do not appear though close at hand.

19   If one befriends a wise and holy being
Who thinks about the truth,[240]
The analytic realization[241]
Of the profound and vast meaning occurs.

20 Show forbearance to the jeering
    Of the hoards of profligates,[242]
    Like an elephant pricked by the archers'
    Sharp arrows [when] drawn up for war.

21 Humans who pierce through their home,
    Have no faith, do not pay back what is made,
    Destroy their chance, and eat vomit —
    They are the holy ones.[243]

22 Those who murder their parents,
    Then overcome king and also saints,
    The country, and all the retinue
    Are said to become purified.[244]

23 Like tracks left by birds in the sky
    It's hard to make out migrations
    Of those who amass nothing at all,
    Who know full well the food,
    And are concerned with detachment,
    And emptiness, and signlessness.[245]

24 Like tracks left by birds in the sky
    It's hard to make out the footprints
    Of those who amass nothing at all,
    Who know full well the food,
    And are concerned with detachment,
    And emptiness, and signlessness.

25 Like tracks left by birds in the sky
    It's hard to make out migrations
    Of those who amass nothing at all,
    Who know full well the food,
    And are always concerned with *samādhi*,
    And emptiness, and signlessness.

26 Like tracks left by birds in the sky
    It's hard to make out the footprints
    Of those who amass nothing at all,
    Who know full well the food,

And are always concerned with *samādhi*,
And emptiness, and signlessness.

27 Like tracks left by birds in the sky
It's hard to make out migrations
Of those who amass nothing at all,
Who know full well the food,
And are concerned with detachment,
And emptiness, and signlessness.[246]

28 Like tracks left by birds in the sky
It's hard to make out the footprints
Of those who amass nothing at all,
Who know full well the food,
And are concerned with detachment,
And emptiness, and signlessness.

29 Like tracks left by birds in the sky
It's hard to make out migrations
Of those without the basis for beyond,
Who know fully contamination's end,
And are concerned with detachment,
And emptiness, and signlessness.

30 Like tracks left by birds in the sky
It's hard to make out the footprints
Of those without the basis for beyond,
Who know fully contamination's end,
And are concerned with detachment,
And emptiness, and signlessness.

31 Like tracks left by birds in the sky
It's hard to make out migrations
Of those without the basis for beyond,
Who know fully contamination's end,
Always concerned with *samādhi*,
And emptiness, and signlessness.

32 Like tracks left by birds in the sky
It's hard to make out the footprints

Of those without the basis for beyond,
Who know fully contamination's end,
Always concerned with *samādhi*,
And emptiness, and signlessness.

33 These ordinary living beings
Are racing into that beyond.
Few are those human beings
Who travel to the other side.

34 Beings who [hear] the excellent doctrine,
And have the view that follows from dharma[247]
Pass over this great sea
Of birth and death that is so hard to cross.

35 The Protector has untied all the knots.
In a state of complete release,
Beyond time and without anguish,
He does not feel sorrow.[248]

36 Passing across the fearful path,
Quitting the precipice for good,
Set free from clasps and knots,
He overcomes the poison of desire.[249]

37 There is no swamp-land like desire.[250]
There is no harmful being like hate.
There is no snare like ignorance.
There is no river like craving.[251]

38 Just as no footprints mark the sky
There are no non-Buddhist religious beings.[252]
Infants like elaborations,
Ones Gone Thus have no liking at all.[253]

39 Since infants are guided by clasps,[254]
Those who are wise destroy them.
The wise who have overcome all
The clasps of humans and the gods,
Are freed from every misery
Since they are free from all clasps.

40   The clasps give rise to existence.[255]
     Without the clasps existence ends.
     Know these two: the way of existence
     And the way of no existence.
     Those who are wise will train
     In order to fully remove the clasps.

41   Sorrow arises from wicked conduct,
     And after bad migration sorrow comes.
     Pleasure arises from good conduct,
     And after good migration pleasure comes.

42   It is better not to do wrong
     Since from that comes two-fold sorrow;
     It's better to have good conduct
     Since sorrow does not come from that.

43   One does not know the infants from the wise
     When silent and mixed together.
     One knows them by their words
     When discoursing about the state of peace.[256]

44   The Seer's ensign is eloquence
     Since the ensign is the dharma.[257]
     By explaining and clarifying it
     Raise up the ensign of the Seer.

45   This world knows nothing but abuse.
     When speaking gently, or even
     When silent or speaking at length,
     There is adverse criticism.

46   Someone abused or praised by all
     Does not exist now at this time,
     And such a one has never been
     And such a one will never be.[258]

47   To the extent they have understood,
     They glorify the flawless[259] ones having faith,
     And ethics, and awareness.
     Like gold ornaments of this world
     Nobody should disparage them.

48   Just as the mountains and the rocks
     Are not made restless by the wind,
     Similarly praise and abuse
     Do not stir up those who are wise.

49   How can there be leaves and stalks
     In a land devoid of roots?[260]
     None should insult that steadfast one
     Discovered to be free from bonds.

50   Though they walk forth, this world with all its gods
     Does not perceive the Mighty, who are free
     From craving, turned from the sorrowful clasp,[261]
     And without the base elaborations.

51   With what and to what state are those
     Unmoving[262] omniscient Buddhas led,
     Whose conquest of the world
     Is complete and knows no decline?

52   With what and to what state are those
     Unmoving omnipotent Buddhas led,
     Whose conquest of the world
     Is complete and knows no decline?

53   With what and to what state are those
     Unmoving omniscient Buddhas led,
     Who have no craving for objects,
     Are free from craving's drawing net?

54   With what and to what state are those
     Unmoving omnipotent Buddhas led,
     Who have no craving for objects,
     Are free from craving's drawing net?

55   Those who have cleared conceptual thought
     And have no inner conceptualizations,
     Are past all clasping, forms, and discrimination,
     Are free from the four yogas, and have no birth.[263]

56   When free from what has gone before,
     From the future, and the middle,
     Beyond craving and free in mind
     One has no further birth and age.

30 *Happiness*

1 From conquest comes vindictiveness.
   Vanquishing others brings misery.
   The happiness of peace is found
   When both of these are given up.[264]

2 Those who, wanting happiness, cause
   Misery to others, befriend
   Their enemies and tormentors
   And aren't released from misery.

3 Those who harm and beat an irksome being
   For their own happiness,
   Want to be happy, but do not
   Find happiness beyond this world.

4 All those who, wanting happiness,
   Don't harm and beat an irksome being,
   Find the happiness they want
   In the world that lies beyond.

5 Do not engage in wicked conduct.
   Engage well in religious conduct.
   Both in this life and future lives
   Religious conduct brings happiness.

6 Engaging well in religious conduct
 Which brings bliss has these benefits:
 One is guarded by that dharma
 And does not go to a bad migration.

7 Like a wide summer parasol,
 Engaging well in religious conduct
 Has these benefits: one is guarded
 And does not go to a bad migration.

8 Any careless migrator goes
 To bad migrations from irreligion.
 Like grasping a black snake by the middle,
 Those who are irreligious are ruined.[265]

9 The fruition of religion
 And irreligion are not the same.
 Irreligion sends one to hell.
 Religion gives good migrations.

10 It is said giving and war are similar.
 From the point of view of time
 And functioning as cause they are alike.
 [The similarity of] these qualities is not based
 On the common person.[266]

11 Just as a solitary, well-armed person
 Scatters and conquers those who're not well armed,
 So too a small gift offered out of faith
 Brings happiness in all those other [lives].[267]

12 Those who resist the foe miserliness,
 And give without attachment in their minds,
 I say these people are greater heroes than
 The champion in one hundred wars.[268]

13 Merit results in happiness,
 The endowment of realizing
 One's wishes, and the quick
 Gaining of holy nirvana.

14 Other[269] noxious influences,
    And heavenly and demonic beings
    Are not able to interfere
    With the effects of making merit.

15 If one who is a Superior
    And has wisdom and benevolence
    Endeavours to end misery,
    It is by insight this is gained.[270]

16 Those who have great faith in their hearts[271]
    And enjoy dharma, find happiness.
    They know and always enjoy the path
    Taught by the Superior ones.

17 Those who enjoy concentrations
    Of mind, enjoy what is not born,[272]
    And the four mindfulnesses,
    The seven branches of enlightenment,
    Enjoy the four miraculous limbs,[273]
    And the eightfold path[274]—
    They wear the monk's robes
    And eat their alms in happiness.[275]
    They stroll in happiness
    Throughout the mountains and the woods,
    They get the happy [path they want]
    And happily achieve nirvana in this life,
    They pass from vindictiveness and fears
    And from the craving of this world.

18 Happiness is to hear and see
    Doctrine and enjoy detachment;
    Happiness is pure vows, and not
    Hurting worldly, irksome beings.

19 Happiness is leaving all desires
    And freedom from attachment to the world
    And supreme is the happiness
    Of those who calm pride in the self.[276]

20 Happiness is ethics in old age.
    Happiness is having a strong faith.
    Happiness is liking meaningful words.
    Happiness is not doing evil deeds.

21 Happiness in this world
    Is adhering[277] to father and mother.
    Happiness in this world is adhering
    To Brahmins and religious persons.

22 Happiness is the advent of Buddhas,
    And the Dharma teachings;
    Happiness is Community in accord,
    And the according austerities.[278]

23 Happiness is seeing those with ethics[279]
    And those who have heard much.
    Happiness is seeing the Foe Destroyers
    Who have been freed from further births.

24 Happy the river in its happy course,[280]
    And happy the Dharma Conqueror.
    Happy the achievement of intelligence,
    Happy the end of pride in self.

25 From seeing Superiors
    And friendship with the holy beings,
    And not seeing infantile beings
    There is continual happiness.

26 Misery comes from friendship
    With infants who are just like an enemy.
    One will regret friendship with them
    For a long time afterwards.

27 A true thoroughbred[281] is a rarity
    Not found everywhere.
    A happiness like meeting relatives
    Comes from befriending [such] steadfast beings.

28 The steadfast ones find happiness

In whatever lineage they are born.[282]
Brahmins who are in nirvana
Engage in total happiness.

29 Those not tainted by desire,
    Without defilement, fully freed,
    Those who have chopped up all craving,
    And cleared infection[283] from the heart,
    Those who attain peace with their minds
    Enter the happiness of nirvana.

30 Wanting extensive happiness
    And wanting to throw off small pleasures,
    The steadfast see extensive happiness
    When small pleasure is given up.

31 Happiness in worlds of desire,
    And the happiness of the heavens,
    Is not the match for a tenth part
    Of the happiness when craving ends.

32 Having taken up a load is misery,
    When it's thrown down there's happiness.[284]
    When burdens are thrown down for good
    They'll not be taken up again.

33 Banish all craving, in order that
    All clasps can be brought to an end.
    If the aggregates are thoroughly known
    One does not go to future lives.

34 Happiness is helpers in a task.
    Happiness is merit at life's end.
    Happiness is contentment with just meagre things,
    And the final sinking down of misery.

35 Just as it is not understood
    How colour leaves the red hot iron
    That gradually cools down
    As it is struck by the hammer,

[Similarly], those who pass from
The soggy swamp-lands of desire,
And attain the unwavering state,
And the excellent liberation
Are not designated migrators.[285]

36   The gods look on but do not comprehend
Those in whose hearts turmoil does not exist:
Fearless, happy, and in nirvana,
Who are turned from craving and non-craving.[286]

37   Someone who has heard much and realized
Dharma, is happy here though destitute,
Seeing how, their minds clinging to [other] beings,
People are ruined through just little things.

38   Those who realize the good in poverty
Are happy here though destitute,
Seeing how, their minds clinging to [other] beings,
People are ruined through just little things.

39   Those who realize the good in poverty
Are happy here though destitute,
Seeing how, clinging to [other] beings' bodies,
People are ruined through just little things.

40   Wretched are those in servitude.
Happy those with independence.
Clasping that is hard to give up
And common to all simply ruins one.[287]

41   To be without attachment
Amongst those who have attachments,
Ah! Not being attached amongst the attached
Is a very happy way to live.[288]

42   To be without sickness[289]
Amongst those stricken with disease,
Ah! Not being sick amongst the sick
Is a very happy way to live.

43   To live without giving injury
    Amongst injurious people,
    Ah! Giving no injury amongst the injurious
    Is a very happy way to live.[290]

44   To be without malice
    Amongst malicious people,
    Ah! Bearing no malice amongst the malicious
    Is a very happy way to live.

45   To be without vindictiveness
    Amongst vindictive people,
    Ah! Forgiveness amongst the vindictive
    Is a very happy way to live.

46   Although [the town of] Mithilā is all ablaze
    Nothing of mine is burning up.[291]
    Ah! I am destitute, which is
    A very happy way to live

47   It's true that I am destitute
    But then, I dine on happiness.
    Ah! Like a god of the Clear Light[292]
    Is a very happy way to live.

48   Freed from the fearful collections,
    It's true that I am destitute.
    Ah! in that I dine on happiness
    It is a very happy way to live.[293]

49   Since attachment,[294] which is the condition
    For connection and contact, is gone,
    In town or wilds, the feelings that arise
    From self and others are not experienced.

50   The pains and pleasures of this world
    Do not affect the holy beings.
    Steadfast, unswayed in the face of desires,
    The holy beings travel everywhere.[295]

31 *The Mind*

1 The mind is hard to grasp, and light,[296]
Going any place it likes;
To calm it down is excellent —
A calm mind leads to peace.

2 When eliminating the base
Of demons,[297] my mind, cast up
From the sea, leaps to and fro —
Just like a fish tossed on the land.

3 Like rays proceeding from the sun
My mind goes racing everywhere.
Like an elephant with a hook
The skilled prevent this happening.[298]

4 I refer to the mind so that
Conduct which has no use to me,
And mind, unseen[299] and essenceless,
Will be forever pacified.

5 Like mahouts do a wild elephant with hooks,
Now work in the right way,[300] hold this mind
That earlier was doing as it pleased,
Chasing about and enjoying itself.

6 It is the housebuilder who caused
   The misery of often taking birth,
   The many cyclic births which
   You have taken, up to now.

7 When you the housebuilder are seen,
   The great beams of the house are all
   Destroyed, the frames all broken up.
   Then housebuilding is done no more.
   The mind is freed from volition,
   This very [birth] accepted as the end.[301]

8 Mind is fickle and moves about,[302]
   It travels off, is hard to stop.
   Secure it with sincerity,
   Like arrowsmiths straighten [arrows] with fire.[303]

9 Whoever pacifies the mind
   That is not form, dwelling within,
   That travels alone and goes far,
   Is liberated from great fears.[304]

10 The mind that has perverted aims
   Causes one greater misery
   Than the hater [does] the hated,
   Than enemies do enemies.

11 The mind that has perfected aims
   Brings happiness to oneself.
   Fathers, mothers, and other friends
   Don't cause such happiness as that.

12 Just as the rain keeps dripping in
   A house that has a damaged roof,
   Desires completely overcome
   The unhabituated mind.[305]

13 Just as the rain does not drip in
   A house with an undamaged roof,
   Desires do not overcome
   The well-habituated mind.

14   Just as the rain keeps dripping in
     A house that has a damaged roof,
     Anger completely overcomes
     The unhabituated mind.

15   Just as the rain does not drip in
     A house with an undamaged roof,
     Anger does not overcome
     The well-habituated mind.

16   Just as the rain keeps dripping in
     A house that has a damaged roof,
     Ignorance completely overcomes
     The unhabituated mind.

17   Just as the rain does not drip in
     A house with an undamaged roof,
     Ignorance does not overcome
     The well-habituated mind.

18   Just as the rain keeps dripping in
     A house that has a damaged roof,
     Pride completely overcomes
     The unhabituated mind.

19   Just as the rain does not drip in
     A house with an undamaged roof,
     Pride does not overcome
     The well-habituated mind.

20   Just as the rain keeps dripping in
     A house that has a damaged roof,
     Attachments completely overcome
     The unhabituated mind.

21   Just as the rain does not drip in
     A house with an undamaged roof,
     Attachments do not overcome
     The well-habituated mind.

22   Just as the rain keeps dripping in

A house that has a damaged roof,
Craving completely overcomes
The unhabituated mind.

23 Just as the rain does not drip in
    A house with an undamaged roof,
    Craving does not overcome
    The well-habituated mind.

24 Thinking mind precedes all phenomena,
    For it is swift and principal.[306]
    Whether it be a word or deed,
    If motivated by vicious thought
    It brings the person misery,
    Like [the man] whose head was cut by the wheel.[307]

25 Thinking mind precedes all phenomena,
    For it is swift and principal.
    Whether it be a word or deed,
    If motivated by a pious thought
    It brings the person happiness,
    Like [the man] followed by the shade.

26 Eloquence is not well understood
    By those who glory in dispute
    And seek with an afflicted mind
    Chances to come out on top.[308]

27 Angry or agitated minds,
    Or minds without faith, are unable
    To comprehend all the holy doctrine
    Which the completed Buddha taught.[309]

28 Whoever calms down wrathfulness,
    And the lack of faith in the mind,
    And banishes malevolence —
    Their [minds] understand eloquence.

29 A mind lacking in constancy
    Does not perceive holy doctrine.

Where faith recedes, wisdom does not
Become completely perfected.

30   Where, [based] on the attachment
To conceptualization,
The streams of the thirty-six horrid views
Gush from the stream of thinking mind,
   [fame declines].[310]

31   The good repute of those who have
Coarse enjoyments and sensibilities
And feeble power of mind grows less,[311]
Like birds in trees stripped of their fruit.

32   Mind, do not delight in ruinous desires,
Be hard working and cautious.
From carelessness you boil in hell.
Don't cry [then] from swallowing the lumps of iron.

33   Those people who sit when it is time to rise,[312]
Stay home and do not work when young and strong,[313]
Who are lazy when their minds mature,
Do not realize the path of wisdom.

34   Because of trifling tiny conceptions
One's inner thought searches out faults.[314]
If those conceptual thoughts are not recognized
Mistaken mind, time and again, goes
   [through cyclic existence].

35   When those with discernment, remembrance,
Perseverance, and skill in conceptions,
Know them, each and every inner thought
Which searches out faults is banished with the mind.[315]

36   Looking upon the body as a pot
And as a city that the mind endures,[316]
Fight and subdue the demons with the sword
Of wisdom, and guard the exclusive place.

37   Looking upon the transient[317] as a pot

And as a city that the mind endures,[318]
Fight and subdue the demons with the sword
Of wisdom, and guard the exclusive place.[319]

38   Looking upon this body as foam
And as a city that the mind endures,
Fight and subdue the demons with the sword
Of wisdom, and guard the exclusive place.

39   Looking upon this world as foam
And as a city that the mind endures,
Fight and subdue the demons with the sword
Of wisdom, and guard the exclusive place.

40   Those whose minds are well conversant
With the seven branches of enlightenment,
Who dislike and banish grasping,
End contamination, and remove
All flaws: such persons pass beyond
The sorrows of every world.

41   Whoever looks after the mind,
Like the yak protects his tail,
And feels affection for irksome beings:
That one's happiness does not decline.

42   The great among the elephants
And elephants long in the tusk —
[Both] rejoice in the woods alone,
Because [Buddha's] mind and
      [the elephant-like] mind are alike.[320]

43   Those without malicious thoughts
And those with love for irksome beings,
Feeling affection for them all,[321]
Encounter no vindictiveness.[322]

44   Those whose minds are without malice
And with love for irksome beings,
Feeling affection for all that live,
Encounter no vindictiveness.

45   Those whose minds are without malice
     And with love for irksome beings,
     Feeling affection for all sentient beings,
     Encounter no vindictiveness.

46   From being a relative and friend to all,
     Feeling affection for irksome beings,
     And cultivating a loving mind,
     Happiness finds great increase.

47   If one feels affection and has no hate
     For any living being, virtue is thereby done.
     A Superior's total merit is achieved
     By having love for every sentient being.

48   Humans who meditate
     With joyful minds and intrepid thought
     On the doctrine of virtue[323]
     Obtain happiness and accomplishments.

49   Right understanding[324] sets one free
     And liberates one from sadness;
     It pacifies one's thoughts
     And the actions of speech and body.

50   Even a five-piece serenade
     Does not give such enjoyment
     As the single-pointed mind
     That sees well all phenomena.[325]

51   Those who enjoy stability[326]
     Of thought don't dally with desires.
     Those Saviours[327] with no anguish
     At all will sleep in happiness.

52   Those who enjoy stability
     Of thought, don't dally with desires.
     The Mighty[328] with no anguish
     At all, Ah! they become happy.

53   How could someone feel miserable
     Whose mind, just like the mountain crag,
     Is deeply unmovable,
     And whose thoughts have become
     Unattached to objects of desire,
     And unmoved by objects of rage?[329]

54   Here is the teaching of Buddha:
     Do not find fault. Do not harm.
     Protect personal liberation vows.
     Understand the amount to eat.
     Cloistered beyond the edge of town,
     Practise the yoga of exalted mind.[330]

55   Those skilled in mental signs,
     Who find the taste of detachment,
     Fully mindful with careful intent,
     Enjoy possessionless pleasure.[331]

56   The sincere, who like and adhere to truth,
     And always guard their physical conduct,
     Their words, and thoughts, give up sorrow
     And don't encounter misery.

57   The minds that are left unguarded
     Are destroyed by perverse views,
     And overcome by sleep and fog
     They fall under the demon's power.[332]

58   Having therefore guarded the mind
     And being led by the right view,
     Pondering the right conceptions[333]
     And knowing right birth and perishing,
     The monk who overcomes sleep and fog
     Attains the end of misery.

59   Happiness is a subdued mind and pure vows.
     Be cautious and protect the mind.
     Those creatures with mistaken minds
     Are sentient beings who burn in hell.

60   Happiness is a subdued mind and pure vows.
     Be cautious and protect the mind.
     Those creatures with mistaken minds
     Burn in the realms of animals.

61   Happiness is a subdued mind and pure vows.
     Be cautious and protect the mind.
     Those creatures with mistaken mind
     Burn in the realms of hungry ghosts.[334]

62   Happiness is a subdued mind and pure vows.
     Be cautious and protect the mind.
     Those creatures who protect the mind
     Enjoy themselves in the realm of humans.

63   Happiness is a subdued mind and pure vows.
     Be cautious and protect the mind.
     Those creatures who protect the mind
     Enjoy themselves in a high rank.

64   Happiness is a subdued mind and pure vows.
     Be cautious and protects the mind.
     Those creatures who protect the mind
     Achieve the state of nirvana.

32 The Monk

1 A monk's alms are just to nourish himself,
   They are not for sustenance of another.
   Gods delight in this refuge who always has
   Remembrance and constant peacefulness.[335]

2 A monk's alms are just to nourish himself,
   They are not for sustenance of another.
   All the gods delight in this refuge,
   Not in those who want wealth and homage and fame.

3 The monk abandons all desires
   And clears the dust that lies before.
   Steadfast great beings [who live by] selflessness
   Do not need to chat with others.[336]

4 Although he hears the odious words
   Spoken in malice by uncontrolled beings,
   The monk free from anger gives them no thought,
   Like elephants at war pricked by arrows.

5 Although he hears the odious words
   Spoken in malice by uncontrolled beings,

The monk, his mind well placed,[337] gives it no
  thought,
Like elephants at war pricked by arrows.

6 A monk does not live by trade,[338] gives up excess,
Likes [to help] himself, is wholly free with senses calm,
Is unattached to home, selfless, and free
Of desire and craving, and works alone.[339]

7 Rely on compatible friends
Who live pure lives and aren't lazy.
Share[340] with each [and everyone]
And be well versed in the forms of conduct.

8 A monk is said to be content,
With good restraint over his arms and legs,
And over all his speech and sense powers,
And to enjoy inner equipoise alone.[341]

9 Monks who take pleasure in doctrine,
Who enjoy and think about doctrine,
And are then mindful of doctrine
Do not fall completely from it.[342]

10 Those monks who live inside
An empty house and look inside [their minds]
And see well[343] all phenomena
Possess the enjoyments of the gods.

11 Happiness and joy are found[344]
To just the same extent
That arising and perishing
Are excellently realized.

12 Monks find the end of misery
By their many happinesses.[345]

13 Just as the wind does not at all
Disturb the craggy mountains,
Monks who have ended desires
Are completely unmoved at all [times].[346]

14 Just as the wind does not at all
    Disturb the craggy mountains,
    So too, monks who have ended hate
    Are completely unmoved at all [times].

15 Just as the wind does not at all
    Disturb the craggy mountains,
    Monks who have ended ignorance
    Are completely unmoved at all [times].

16 Just as the wind does not at all
    Disturb the craggy mountains,
    So too, monks who have ended pride
    Are completely unmoved at all [times].

17 Just as the wind does not at all
    Disturb the craggy mountains,
    Monks who have ended attachments
    Are completely unmoved at all [times].

18 Just as the wind does not at all
    Disturb the craggy mountains,
    Monks who have ended craving
    Are completely unmoved at all [times].

19 He is said to be a 'monk'
    Who does not gather anything,
    Does not treat anything as 'mine'
    And feels no pain though destitute.[347]

20 One who just begs from others now and then,
    On reflection is not, I think, a monk.
    One who holds on to city things,
    On reflection is not, I think, a monk.[348]

21 A 'monk' is said to be the one
    Who is virtuous and banishes
    Wrongs, has pure conduct, and gives up
    Society[349] and does the work.

22 Any monk who is kind,[350] and has

Complete faith in the Buddha's teaching
Achieves the state of peace,
The seeing of which will never pall.[351]

23 Any monk who is kind, and has
Complete faith in the Buddha's teaching
Finds the state of peacefulness
Where composites[352] are pacified.

24 Any monk who is kind, and has
Complete faith in the Buddha's teaching
Gradually experiences
The end of every clasping.

25 Any monk who is kind, and has
Complete faith in the Buddha's teaching
Extracts himself from bad rebirths,
Like an elephant from the mud.

26 Any monk who is kind, and has
Complete faith in the Buddha's teaching
Shakes out all evil phenomena,[353]
Like wind shakes out the leaves from trees.

27 Any monk who is kind, and has
Complete faith in the Buddha's teaching
Can not fully degenerate
Because he is close to liberation.

28 That monk with joyful mind and pure thoughts
Who overcomes likes and dislikes,
Will by his many joys
Achieve the end of misery.

29 Body and speech at peace, and mind at peace
And in excellent equipoise:
The monk who gives up worldly goods
Is called 'the one in constant peace'.[354]

30 Without stability there is no wisdom,
Without wisdom, no stability.

The ones who have stability
And wisdom are to be called 'monks'.[355]

31 Since stability and wisdom
Are thus the object of the wise,
Similarly, the first labour
Of intelligent monks is these.

32 Here is the teaching of the Buddha:
Being content, control your senses,
Protect personal liberation vows,
Understand the amount to eat,
Cloistered beyond the edge of town
Practise the yoga of exalted mind.[356]

33 A monk is one whose body and whose speech
And thoughts are not engaged in wrong.
He has a sense of shame
And holds to virtuous ethics.

34 Because he has the virtuous aspect,
Cultivating well the seven
Factors of complete enlightenment,
[One] in equipoise is called 'monk'.[357]

35 Because he fully knows the end
Of personal misery here,
Is virtuous and has wisdom,
The uncontaminated one is called 'monk'.[358]

36 Unless they have attained the end
Of contamination, those with just
Ethics and conduct,[359] or much hearing,
Or those who dwell in solitude,
Or gain stability yet grow tired,
Are not monks in the deepest sense.[360]

37 The worldly beings who say
'I' of the aggregates suffer.
Superiors steadfastly actualize
The bliss of complete enlightenment.[361]

38 To the extent they think [differently],
    The [Superiors] become different from [ordinary
        beings].362

39 Worldly beings who become different,
    Are attached to and like and have
    Pronounced attachment to the world,
    They look on and like the world itself.
    That which [ordinary beings] like is misery.
    That which they fear is happiness.363

40 So in order to banish the world
    [Superiors] conduct themselves purely in this
        [dharma].

41 All [such] Brahmins and religious persons
    Are called 'renouncers of the world'.364
    All other [ordinary beings] are called
    'Those who have not renounced the world'.

42 All Brahmins and religious persons
    Are called 'liberated from the world'.
    All other [ordinary beings] are called
    'Those not liberated from the world'.

43 Taking conditions misery,
    And from misery comes taking.
    If taking is completely finished,
    Then misery does not arise.365

If all aspects of existence, [all taking], are seen with perfect
wisdom actually as they are: 'impermanent, [in the nature of]
misery and completely changeable', all craving for existence is
banished. When existence is no more there is joy.366 The
Saviour, the monk in nirvana, having no taking at another
[time],367 does not take a future existence. For he has
overcome the demons, and is victorious in battle. A complete
transcendence of all existence such as this is the end of misery.

44 The monk who cuts the functioning [cause],
    Peaceful, and with peace of mind,

Does not take future birth.
He has abandoned the cycle of births.

45 The monk who cuts the functioning [cause],
Peaceful, and with peace of mind,
Is liberated from the demon's chains.[368]
He has abandoned the cycle of births.

46 The monk who cuts the functioning [cause],
Whose mind becomes uncontaminated,
Does not take future birth.
He has abandoned the cycle of births.

47 The monk who cuts the functioning [cause],
Whose mind becomes uncontaminated,
Is liberated from the demon's chains.
He has abandoned the cycle of births.

48 The monk who cuts the functioning [cause],
Who chops up craving for existence,
Does not take future birth.
He has abandoned the cycle of births.

49 The monk who cuts the functioning [cause],
Who chops up craving for existence,
Is liberated from the demon's chains.
He has abandoned the cycle of births.

50 Whoever excellently fords the swamp,[369]
Cuts down the thorns of the town
And is beyond[370] the ending of desire:
This is the [person] called a monk.

51 Whoever excellently fords the swamp,
Cuts down the thorns of the town
And is beyond the ending of anger:
This is the [person] called a monk.

52 Whoever excellently fords the swamp,
Cuts down the thorns of the town
And is beyond the end of ignorance:
This is the [person] called a monk.

53   Whoever excellently fords the swamp,
     Cuts down the thorns of the town
     And is beyond the ending of pride:
     This is the [person] called a monk.

54   Whoever excellently fords the swamp,
     Cuts down the thorns of the town
     And is beyond the end of attachment:
     This is the [person] called a monk.

55   Whoever excellently fords the swamp,
     Cuts down the thorns of the town
     And is beyond the ending of craving:
     This is the person called a monk.

56   A monk calms scolding and killing,
     Restraining and the thorns of the town.
     Unmoved by pain and happiness,
     Mountain-like he is not led astray.

57   Those monks[371] who neither deny nor fabricate
     [Truth], and know the entire world is deceptive,
     Go beyond and cast off what's not beyond
     Like old serpents shedding old skin.

58   Those monks who calm desire that arises,
     Like medicine [does] the poison of a snake,[372]
     Go beyond and leave what is not beyond
     Like old serpents shedding old skin.

59   Those monks who calm hatred that arises,
     Like medicine the poison of a snake,
     Go beyond and leave what is not beyond
     Like old serpents shedding old skin.

60   Those monks who calm ignorance that arises,
     Like medicine the poison of a snake,
     Go beyond and leave what is not beyond
     Like old serpents shedding old skin.

61   Those monks who calm pride that arises,

Like medicine the poison of a snake,
Go beyond and leave what is not beyond
Like old serpents shedding old skin.

62 Those monks who calm attachment that arises,
Like medicine the poison of a snake,
Go beyond and leave what is not beyond
Like old serpents shedding old skin.

63 Those monks who calm anger that arises,
Like medicine the poison of snake,
Go beyond and leave what is not beyond
Like old serpents shedding old skin.

64 Those monks who calm craving that arises,
Like medicine the poison of a snake,
Go beyond and leave what is not beyond
Like old serpents shedding old skin.

65 Those monks who eradicate all desire,
Like a mighty flood a weak dam,
Go beyond and leave what is not beyond
Like old serpents shedding old skin.[373]

66 Those monks who eradicate all anger,
Like a mighty flood a weak dam,
Go beyond and leave what is not beyond
Like old serpents shedding old skin.

67 Those monks who eradicate all ignorance,
Like a mighty flood a weak dam,
Go beyond and leave what is not beyond
Like old serpents shedding old skin.

68 Those monks who eradicate all pride,
Like a mighty flood a weak dam,
Go beyond and leave what is not beyond
Like old serpents shedding old skin.

69 Those monks who eradicate all attachment,
Like a mighty flood a weak dam,

Go beyond and leave what is not beyond
Like old serpents shedding old skin.

70   Those monks who eradicate all craving,
Like a mighty flood a weak dam,
Go beyond and leave what is not beyond
Like old serpents shedding old skin.

71   Those monks who leave the objects of desire,
And clear away the chains of desire's clasp,
Go beyond and leave what is not beyond
Like old serpents shedding old skin.

72   Those monks who abandon all obscuration,
And without wrongs cut the pain of doubt,[374]
Go beyond and leave what is not beyond
Like old serpents shedding old skin.

73   Those monks who clear away concepts, free from
All inner conceptualization,[375]
Go beyond and leave what is not beyond
Like old serpents shedding old skin.[376]

74   Those monks without any jungle,[377]
Who have pulled up the root of non-virtue,
Go beyond and leave what is not beyond
Like old serpents shedding old skin.

75   Those monks free from all contagious disease,[378]
Who have pulled up the root of non-virtue,
Go beyond and leave what is not beyond
Like old serpents shedding old skin.

76   Those monks without any latencies,
Who have pulled up the root of non-virtue,
Go beyond and leave what is not beyond
Like old serpents shedding old skin.

77   Monks are those who have ethics.
Concentrators are those with emptiness.
Yogis are those who always do that [work].
Those in nirvana are the Blissful Ones.[379]

78 A monk does not speak out of love or hate,
    He keeps his seat beyond the edge of town.
    He is cautious, and excellently
    Eradicates all desire for the world.[380]

33 *The Brahmin*

1 Brahmins, religious beings, and monks
   Are, though wearing jewels, religious and calm,
   Are peaceful, have pure vows and work purely,
   And cause no harm to any irksome being.[381]

2 It is not going naked, the knots of hair, the baldness;[382]
   It is not abstaining from food nor sleeping on the
      ground;
   It is not dust nor dirt, the squatting postures in which
      they struggle
   That purify humans, and take them past uncertainty.[383]

3 Whether [called] Brahmins or religious people,
   All of these selves have attachment
   And don't attain the end of contamination.
   They sink into the middle world.[384]

4 Whether [called] Brahmins or religious people,
   All of these selves[385] have attachment.
   They sink into the middle world
   And don't attain the end of feeling.[386]

5 Whether [called] Brahmins or religious people,

All of these selves have attachment.
Holding the extreme views of infants
They sink into the middle world.[387]

6   Whether [called] Brahmins or religious people,
All of these selves have attachment.
Having the vile mind of infantile beings
They sink into the middle world.

7   Whether [called] Brahmins or religious people,
All of these selves have attachment.
They sink into the middle world.
And don't attain the holy place.

8   You with vile minds! Why knot your hair,
And why wear deerskin clothes,
Presenting such a spotless front
While the murk remains within?[388]

9   You with vile minds! Why knot your hair
And why wear deerskin clothes?
Presenting such a spotless front
While the stains remain within.

10   Brahmins do not arise because of caste,
Because of knots of hair or lineage.
Those who possess truth and dharma[389]
Are the clean ones: they are Brahmins.

11   Brahmins do not arise because of caste,
Because of knots of hair or lineage.
Because they eliminate all wrongs,
All people who eliminate
Each and every wrong, great and small,
Should be known as Brahmins.

12   Shaved heads do not produce religious beings,
Nor chanting Oṃ produce Brahmins.
Those who possess the virtuous dharma
Are the clean ones: they are Brahmins.

13 Shaved heads do not produce religious beings,
    Nor chanting *Om* produce Brahmins.
    Because they eliminate all wrongs,
    All people who eliminate
    Each and every wrong, great and small,
    Are Brahmins [and] religious beings.

14 The water does not purify
    Most of the people washing here.[390]
    Because they eliminate all wrongs,
    It is people who eliminate
    Each and every wrong, great and small,
    Who are Brahmins [and] religious beings.

15 The Buddha who ended clasping,
    Who eliminated every wrong,
    And always has remembrance as he works
    Is the Brahmin of every world.[391]

16 The Brahmin who eliminates wrongdoing,
    Without guile and upset remains himself,
    Completes the Vedic [path], and works purely,
    Is in one context spoken of as *Brahman*.[392]

17 Brahmins, religious beings, and monks
    Do not harbour deceit or pride,
    Have no attachment, self or hopes,
    Overcome strife and are near nirvana.

18 Let those born from a mother's womb,
    If they have a recitation,
    Be named for what they say.
    I do not call those 'Brahmin'.[393]

19 A Brahmin, I say, is one
    Without adherence and grasping.

20 A Brahmin, I say, is one
    Who controls well the three grounds
    And never does anything bad
    With body, speech and mind.

21 A Brahmin, I say, is one
Whose speech is pleasing to the ear,
Meaningful, and without harshness,
And does not create afflictions.

22 A Brahmin, I say, is one
With an accumulated power of restraint,[394]
Who has forbearance, and does not kill,
Tie up, scold or feel hatred.

23 A Brahmin, I say, is one
Without anger, keeping ethics,
Who is self-trained, has no wrong,
Is calm and in the last body.

24 A Brahmin, I say, is one
With few desires, who has left home,
Who does not associate with monks,
Or laity, or likewise with both.[395]

25 A Brahmin, I say, is one
Victorious, free from the clasps of sex,
Without liking for what is to come,
And without anguish from the past.[396]

26 A Brahmin, I say, is one
Without liking for what is to come,
And past anguish, is at peace,
Free from dust and without pain.

27 A Brahmin, I say, is one
Who has few needs, not keeping others,[397]
And is subdued; [a Brahmin] abides at the heart,
Uncontaminated and faultless.

28 A Brahmin, I say, is one
Gone past [desire] for all phenomena,
For whom there is not here nor there,
Nor here and there combined.[398]

29 A Brahmin, I say, is one
Unattached to the three places,

For whom there is not here nor there,
Nor here and there combined.

30 A Brahmin, I say, is one
Who does not grasp long and short,
Subtle or rough, non-virtue or virtue;
Not the littlest bit of the world.[399]

31 A Brahmin, I say, is one
Who knows well [the abandonment of] these;
Who has ended misery, and is
Free from attachment and without
   [afflictive emotions].

32 A Brahmin, I say, is one
Untainted by virtues and wrongs,
And by them both combined;[400] untainted,
Free from dust and at peace.

33 A Brahmin, I say, is one
Free and passed beyond attachment,
Completely beyond attachment
To virtue and wrong-doing.

34 A Brahmin, I say, is one
Free from dust, released from bonds,
Who is not earlier nor later,
Nor in between [these two times].[401]

35 A Brahmin, I say, is one
In whom wrongdoing has no place,
Like water on lotus petals,
Like mustard seed on the tip of the ripened
   mustard plant.[402]

36 A Brahmin, I say, is one
In whom desire has no place,
Like water on lotus petals,
Like mustard seed on the tip of the ripened
   mustard plant.

37   A Brahmin, I say, is one
     Who gives up liking for the world,
     Like water on lotus petals,
     Like mustard seed on the tip of the ripened
        mustard plant.

38   A Brahmin, I say, is one
     Who is untainted by wrongdoing.
     Like the perfect, unflawed clarity[403]
     Of the stainless, sublime moon.

39   A Brahmin, I say, is one
     Who is untainted by desires,
     Like the perfect, unflawed clarity
     Of the stainless, sublime moon.

40   A Brahmin, I say, is one
     Who gives up liking for the world,
     Like the perfect, unflawed clarity
     Of the stainless, sublime moon.

41   A Brahmin, I say, is one
     Who is untainted by wrongdoing.
     Like the swamps are to the sun,
     As the dust is to the moon.

42   A Brahmin, I say, is one
     Who is untainted by desires,
     Like the swamps are to the sun,
     As the dust is to the moon.

43   A Brahmin, I say, is one
     Who gives up liking for the world,
     Like the swamps are to the sun,
     As the dust is to the moon.

44   A Brahmin, I say, is one
     Who seated, has become free from dust,
     Who thinks, does the work, and ends contamination,
     Is calmed, and in the final body.[404]

45 A Brahmin, I say, is one
   Who has profound wisdom and sincere thought,
   Skilled in what is and what is not the path,
   And with the best post-meditation state.[405]

46 This person could be any human being
   Who lives on alms alone, is selfless,[406]
   And does not hurt a single thing.
   A Brahmin, I say, is one who,
   Steadfast and doing the pure work,
   Teaches doctrine in virtue of being all-knowing.

47 A Brahmin, I say, is one
   Who, leaving home and taking vows,
   Excellently eliminates desires,
   And stops desire's contamination.[407]

48 A Brahmin, I say, is one
   Who does not kill or order death,
   Who does no harm to irksome beings
   Which move or remain still.[408]

49 A Brahmin, I say, is one
   Who helps[409] and loves enemies, facing
   The unwarranted with equanimity
   And accepting any violence.

50 A Brahmin, I say, is one
   Like mustard seed on the tip of the ripened mistard
      plant,
   Who overcomes desire,
   Anger, and pride and attachment.

51 Completely beyond craving's citadel,[410]
   Beyond the river of this cyclic world,
   A Brahmin, I say, is one
   Travelling to the farther shore,
   Untrammelled by uncertainty,
   Mindful, and turned back from craving.

52 A Brahmin, I say, is one

Who has completely stopped craving
For existence, without craving
For this or for a future world.

53 A Brahmin, I say, is one
Free from longing,[411] emancipated,
Without attachment to
This world or to the [world] beyond.

54 A Brahmin, I say, is one
Free from dislikes and likes,
Who is cooled down, uncontaminated,
Steadfastly eclipsing the entire world.[412]

55 A Brahmin, I say, is one
Set free from every clasp,
Free from the clasps of all humans,
Quite past the clasps of the gods.

56 A Brahmin, I say, is one
At peace who doesn't know life:
Not knowing the life of gods,
Of *Gandharvas*,[413] or the life of humans.

57 A Brahmin, I say, is one
Who views limitless phenomena,
From whom not knowing, or not seeing[414]
Of all phenomena is gone.

58 Knowing the places of the past,
Seeing heaven and bad migrations,
A Brahmin, I say, is one
Who then perseveres at the Conquerors'
Clairvoyance which gains the end of births,
And knows well the last misery.[415]

59 A Brahmin, I say, is one
Who knows the liberation of the mind,
Who is free from all desires,
And has the three knowledges.[416]

60 A Brahmin, I say, is one

With unrestricted sight, a Buddha
Who knows every being's birth
And where each goes at death.

61 A Brahmin, I say, is one
Completely beyond all craving,
A mindful teacher without pleasure,
For whom there is no great anguish.

62 A Brahmin, I say, is a
Great elephant, first amongst leaders,
An untrammelled, pure Buddha,
A mighty and victorious saint.[417]

63 A Brahmin, I say, is one
Passed from the world, eclipsing all,
Beyond the river, an emancipator
Gone to the farther shore and freed.

64 A Brahmin, I say, is a
Thinker who sits and is self-freed from dust.
This one does not think about,
Meditate on, and talk of wrongs.[418]

65 A Brahmin, I say, is one
Who lives beneath the trees,
Modest, not gazing on desires,
Wearing clothes of cast-off rags.[419]

66 A Brahmin, I say, is one
Who, to eliminate all misery,
Cultivates the straightforward,
Peaceful, eightfold noble path.[420]

67 A Brahmin, I say, is one
For whom nothing at all remains,[421]
All-knowing, without doubts or pains,
Beholding the stage of immortality.

68 A Brahmin, I say, is one
Who subdues the hard-to-subdue mind

That is not form, dwelling within,
That travels alone and goes far.[422]

69 The Brahmins of this world are those [whose minds]
Are formless, unshowable, and limitless,
Quite unseen, subtle, a basis, realized,
Awake, always mindful and free from clasps.[423]

70 A Brahmin, I say, is one
Who cuts the cords and mesh.
Having cut the tightened cords
This one abandons anguish and awakes.[424]

71 A Brahmin, I say, is one
Who tears out craving and its root,
Cutting through the cords and mesh,
Through wanting goods and doing wrong.

72 A Brahmin is one who does no wrong,
Works hard and cuts the river's flow,
Completely overcomes desires
And knows the end of all compounds.

73 A Brahmin is one who does no wrong.
Murdering the parents, this one then
Overcomes king and both saints,
The country and all the retinue.[425]

74 A Brahmin is one who does no wrong.
Murdering parents, this one then
Oversomes king and both saints
And slays the fierce tiger.[426]

75 Do not ever hit a Brahmin;
Do not drive Brahmins away.
Those who strike Brahmins are fools,
And whoever drives them out is bad.[427]

76 As the saintly Brahmin does the fire,
One worships and bows down before
Those people, be they young or old,
Who are conscious[428] of all phenomena.

77 As the saintly Brahmin does the fire,
    One worships and makes offerings to
    Those people, be they young or old,
    Who are conscious of all phenomena.

78 As the saintly Brahmin does the fire,
    One worships and bows down before
    The people who are conscious
    Of all phenomena that Buddha taught.

79 As the saintly Brahmin does the fire,
    One worships and makes offerings to
    The people who are conscious
    Of all phenomena that Buddha taught.

80 When a Brahmin becomes perfect
    In [the mode] of all phenomena,
    That one even leaves behind
    The [terrifying] spirit of Bakula.[429]

81 When a Brahmin becomes perfect
    In [the mode] of all phenomena,[430]
    With that there is seeing, and all
    [Worldly] feelings disappear.[431]

82 When a Brahmin becomes perfect
    In [the mode] of all phenomena,
    Then, with that there is seeing,
    And all conditions disappear.[432]

83 When a Brahmin becomes perfect
    In [the mode] of all phenomena,
    Then, with that there is seeing,
    And all clasping[433] disappears.

84 When a Brahmin becomes perfect
    In [the mode] of all phenomena,
    That one completely leaves all birth,
    Old age, and death behind.

85 Just as the sun shines out in the day,

Just as the moon appears at night,
Just as the king's armour shines out amongst the
   troops,
The mind of the Brahmin shines out.[434]

86   Just as the sun shines out in the day,
Just as the moon appears at night,
Through day and night, the resplendent
Buddha perpetually shines forth.[435]

87   A Brahmin never has anything like
Revulsion for unpleasantness.
To the extent there is revulsion
There is the ending of relative truths.[436]

88   When a Brahmin with diligence and thought,[437]
Emerging well from all this religion,[438]
Understands well phenomena and cause[439]
Then that one is freed from every doubt.

89   When a Brahmin with diligence and thought,
Emerging well from all this religion,
Understands well misery and the cause[440]
Then that one is freed from every doubt.

90   When a Brahmin with diligence and thought,
Emerging well from all this religion,
Attains the finish of all conditions[441]
Then that one is freed from every doubt.

91   When a Brahmin with diligence and thought,
Emerging well from all this religion,
Attains the finishing of all feelings
Then that one is freed from every doubt.

92   When a Brahmin with diligence and thought,
Emerging well from this religion,
Attains the finish of contamination[442]
Then that one is freed from every doubt.

93   When, like the sun arising in the sky,

A Brahmin, through diligence and thought
Is present, appearing to all the world,
That one has emerged well from all religion.

94   When a Brahmin, with diligence and thought,
Is freed from all clasps by the mind,
Is present [in a state] free from demons,
That one has emerged well from all religion.[443]

Notes

1. W. Woodville Rockhill, trans., *Udānavarga: A Collection of Verses From the Buddhist Canon,* (Trübner's Oriental Series, Calcutta) 1892. Reprinted 1982, distributed by D.K. Publishers' Distributers, New Delhi. A translation of the Tibetan *Ched du brjod pa'i tshoms.*
2. Rockhill, Introduction p.xi.

1 Impermanence

3. 'Relate correctly' indicates that the verses are authentic teachings of the Buddha. Dharmatrāta is only the compiler.
4. Tib: *bcom ldan 'das.* The Victorious One who has overcome all obstacles and by abandoning all causes of misery, gone beyond it.
5. The first two verses are an exhortation by the compiler. The Buddha's first teaching on the four noble truths, reported in his own words, begins with the third verse.
6. Prajñāvarman's *Commentary* says that when the Buddha awoke to find the monks much enamoured of a new rest house that they had been given, he spoke this verse.
7. Rockhill, p.4 footnote 1, prefers *dga' ba* (joy) to *dka' ba* (difficulty).
8. 'Since in the future [life] I don't exist' is another possible reading.

9. Tib: *sems.*

10. At one time the Buddha was sitting outside in the sun; a monk saw him and admired the perfection of his body. The Buddha then spoke these words.

11. This verse, which is not found in *Com.*, appears to be an addition to the text.

12. Tib: *mi thogs.* This can be understood in the sense that nobody stops it happening.

13. All the faults and sorrow taught in the earlier verses cause a dislike for cyclic existence. 'So' refers to the dislike.

2   Desire

14. *Com.* explains that pain occurs when what is desired is lost, while fear results from losing what has been obtained.

15. Generally, *gong 'pho ba*—'One Who Ascends'—refers to a Non-returner, not to a Foe Destroyer. Here, however, the name is best applied to the latter (see Intro. p. 13). The first line presents some difficulties. The *bKa' 'gyur* edition of *Compilations* reads, *dun pa skyes shing zad par mi byed dam; Com.* reads, *zag par mi byed dang.* An alternative translation is '[the Foe Destroyer] does not end his or her longing [for nirvana]'.

    Com. says 'contaminate' means to drip, as from an open orifice. Thus the ordained person without good ethics is unable to control the doors of the senses and his or her consciousness leaks out and contaminates all the objects of desire.

16. Tib: *sred pa,* 'craving' is from *Com.; bKa' 'gyur* has *srid pa,* 'world'.

17. Rockhill p.11 quotes Wilson, *Sanskrit Dictionary* p. 199 'A weight of gold or silver equal to sixteen *marshas.*'

3   Craving

18. Line one: *'dra* means 'like'; *dra* means 'net'. The alternative translation of the first line would then be 'Enveloped by the net of murky desire'. This is also a suitable reading because of the example of the fish used in the last line. *Com.* considers both readings. Line two: *dga' ba* means liking; *dgab ba* means to cover. *Com.* considers only the latter. Craving covers and obscures the mind, precluding interest in the attainment of liberation. Tib: *tsed ma,* in the last line, is explained both as

meaning a net or a stick for spearing fish.

19. I.e. craving grows where there is carelessness, like a vine on a tree.

19a. Kantipālo Thera, *Buddhist Studies Review* 1, 2 (1983-4) suggests a better translation of *byis pa* (Skt. *bāla*) is 'fools'. On purely literary grounds he is correct, but, since the term *byis pa* refers to people who (like children) innocently believe in the reality of what they see and hear the translation 'infant' is retained.

20. Tib: *kun sbyor*, clasp, is explained in *Com.* as follows. 'A clasp' is an afflictive emotion (found throughout the three realms). Liking for cyclic existence arises because of a clasp. There are four clasps: desire, existence, belief and ignorance.

21. The dew drop simply sits on the lotus but never penetrates to the centre nor saturates the petals. The lotus is the mind.

22. Tib: *len pa*, attachment, the ninth link in the wheel of dependent arising. See Intro. pp.21-23.

23. 'Monk', throughout the book, generally is synonymous with a Foe Destroyer who is not a householder. Tib: *kun tu rgyu* means to 'wander everywhere'. The non-householder monk or nun is often an itinerant religious person. The *Com.* suggests that in this present instance, the phrase should also be taken as a reference to attainment of non-residual nirvana.

4 Caution

24. The *Com.* says this verse teaches the five powers; the first four—effort, remembrance, stability, and wisdom—are considered the cause of the fifth power, faith. This faith, like an island of rock in the middle of a great river, cannot be swept away.

25. This verse is dealt with later in *Com.* It says the first two lines teach the three higher trainings in ethics, stabilization and wisdom and the last two their result. Tib: *thub pa'i thub gzhi*, literally 'becoming of kings'. 'Kings' here is equivalent to Foe Destroyers. The jumbled order of the verses may perhaps have arisen because of the distinctly Mahāyānist flavour of some of the terminology.

26. 'Worldly view', the view which is common to all virtuous people of the world, is ethics.

27. *Com.* says 'the female beast' could be either an actual bird or animal, or a mythical creature. It is said to follow the lion, licking it with its tongue. The enjoyment the lion derives from this sends it to sleep, whereon the 'female beast' pecks or gores out its eyes.
28. 'The body nature' refers to the object of one of the four close mindfulnesses or remembrances. The objects of observation are the body, feelings, mind and phenomena.
29. 'The work' of becoming a Foe Destroyer.
30. The two states are nirvana with and without remainder.
31. These six verses posit the difference between the Buddhist and non-Buddhist paths. The latter do not serve as an antidote to the subtle and rough afflictions which cause birth in the form and formless realms. The attainments of a non-Buddhist path, therefore, are always attained within cyclic existence and are subject to degeneration.

5   Beauty

32. It is possible that this stanza was inserted into or changed from the original. It differs in many respects from the version under consideration in *Com.*, although the basic meaning appears to be the same.
33. 'Demon-food'; *Com.* says, whoever has desires, has death; on whomever has food, the vultures descend.
34. For *Com. sdig pa,* 'wrongdoing', text has *sdug pa,* 'beauty'.
35. This verse comes three stanzas later in the *bKa' 'gyur.* The order here follows *Com.*
36. Tib: *gnas,* 'ground', means a skilful cause, i.e. virtue. A 'non ground' or 'ungrounded' would mean an unskilful cause, such as a blood sacrifice. These activities are thought to be a cause of happiness but are not so.
37. *Com.* says dharma is compassion; i.e. kindness.

6   Ethics

38. See note 36 for the meaning of *gnas,* 'ground'. This verse was said by Buddha during the confession ceremony when a monk felt offended. The wise do not become offended when their faults are pointed out and when they are taught how to meditate.
39. This verse defines ethics as that which brings relief. By

keeping ethics there is no physical pain from being punished and no mental pain from apprehensiveness, etc. Keeping ethics thus becomes the cultivation of contentment.

40. The phrase 'parting from mind' points to the path of seeing. The path of seeing is the means for removing the causes of rebirth. 'Ending the rest' indicates the paths of meditation and no more learning. Relying on these, all the remaining obstacles are eliminated.

41. 'Shine out radiant'. This verse comprises the answer the Buddha gave to a sun-worshipper who asked, 'Who in all the world outshines the sun?'

42. This verse also was directed towards the worshipper of the sun.

43. Rockhill, quoting Childer's *Pali Dictionary* says, '*Mallikā* is jasmine.'

7 *Fine Conduct*

44. The four immeasurables are: immeasurable love, compassion, joy and equanimity.

45. 'Mighty' is an epithet of the Buddha.

46. Tib: *thub ga*, 'might' and 'sage', those free from attachment, i.e. Superiors.

47. 'Steadfast' means wise ordinary beings.

8 *Words*

48. Forty-one thousand would be multiplied by ten million in which case the result of such scorn would be about forty billion years. Rockhill labels the hells '*nirabbudas*' and '*abbudas*'.

9 *Actions*

49. *Com.* relates this verse to an altercation between two kings, Prasenajit and Ajātaśatru. When the former asked of Buddha whether he should incarcerate and execute Ajātaśatru, whom he had beaten in battle and captured, the Buddha replied that he should not. This verse refers to what was said at that time.

10. *Faith*

50. Each earlier quality leads to the next.

51. 'The best of all tastes....' teaches ethics. The *Com.* advises

interpreting 'truth' here as the faith which inspires or causes ethics.

52. 'Religion' in this instance stands for giving. The importance of giving is included in the verses about faith, because just as fire is known from smoke, faithlessness is known from miserliness.

53. Because faith motivates one to listen, faith is taught as a cause of intelligence.

54. The line about 'caution' signifies the path of seeing, that of 'faith' signifies the cause of the path of seeing, that of 'effort' signifies the path of meditation, and that of 'wisdom', the path of no more learning.

55. The first three lines of this verse can be understood as referring to the lineages of the Buddha, the Hearer, and the Solitary Realizer.

11   The Ordained Person

56. Tib: *kun tu rgyu*, 'itinerant'. See note 23.

57. This follows *Com*. The *bKa' 'gyur* differs and is probably incorrect.

58. Confessing wrongs again and again is seen as a method to achieve good conduct and calm mind.

59. This line can be taken to refer to 'house dwellers' or 'house-holders'; the line would then read 'House dwellers who undertake wrong'.

60. Buddha said this verse to an old Brahmin to show that a person is ranked as a venerable not from caste or age, but from the religious work that has been done.

61. 'Future crowd' means next life. An 'ultimate venerable' is therefore a person in nirvana, working for others before death.

62. There are eight true Superiors. See Intro. pp.25-26. This verse refers to the first seven types, that is, those who are 'relative' superior persons.

63. The last verse in this section explains the Foe Destroyer, the ultimate Superior or ordained person. This explains the various meanings of what is synonymous with religious person.

12   The Path

64. In the Vaibhāṣika system the first fifteen instants of non-conceptual meditation on the four truths are considered to be path of seeing and the sixteenth instant is the path of

meditation. The third line teaches the path of meditation.

65. There are four stages of realizations on the path of preparation. The last stage is the definite bringer of the path of seeing and therefore is called the finest or foremost of worldly intelligence.

66. The eightfold path of Superiors is likened to a wheel. Through his own realization of this path, or state of mind, characterized by advanced stability, intelligence, effort etc., Buddha was able to teach this path of achievement to others. He taught in such a way that it came into being in the listener's mind. His 'turning the wheel of Dharma' is setting in motion the hearing, understanding, practising, and passing on of this religious doctrine. The wheel of the eightfold path turns in the sense that it moves or revolves as a living practice in the minds of those who achieve the path of seeing.

67. The three virtuous concepts are: renunciation, love and compassion. All non-virtuous conceptual states of mind are included in the opposites of these three: longing-desire, malice and unkindness. To pass from the realm of desire to the first concentration in the realm of form, the conceptual non-virtues must be calmed. To pass from the first to the second concentration, the coarse conceptualization (which exists only in the simple practice of the first concentration) and the subtle conceptualization (which exists also in the special practice), must both be eliminated. Both coarse and subtle conceptualization form or deal with the virtuous states. To move from the actual first concentration to the second concentration, all states of mind included in the first concentration, including the virtuous conceptualizations, are eliminated. Different virtuous conceptualizations included in the second concentration are then practised that eliminate certain undesirable types of joy and happiness. See Intro.

68. 'Unsurpassed enlightenment' in this instance indicates freedom from craving.

69. This can be taken to mean either the three doors to liberation or the above three stabilizations (see note 67)—the one with both rough and subtle conceptualizations, the one without the former, and the one without both.

70. *Com.* has 'born from detachment'.

71. 'The three places' could be either the three realms or three bad migrations. 'These three' could be the above stabilizations or three higher trainings.

13 *Honours*

72. 'White part' is the name of the first of the four divisions of the
    path of preparation.
73. 'Increase' means to cultivate; 'detachment' means the eightfold
    path.
74. These verses teach the four traits of a person of superior
    lineage: contentment with simple robes, contentment with
    simple food and drink given as alms, contentment with a
    meagre sleeping place, and enjoyment of doing what is to be
    done and eliminating what is to be eliminated.
75. 'To view things as a religious person' is, here, the equivalent of
    achieving a Superior's path of seeing.
76. This line may also be read as 'And meditate on one dharma';
    'one dharma' then refers to the four close mindfulnesses.
77. This would be the result of not broadcasting one's own good
    qualities.
78. The three knowledges are: knowledge of previous places of
    birth, of death and rebirth, and of uncontaminated
    phenomena.
79. 'Mindfulness' is the four close mindfulnesses of body etc.;
    'monk-(hood)' is nirvana with remainder; 'the full going'
    nirvana without remainder.
80. 'Subtle pain' is the misery occurring from the degeneration of
    one's good qualities. This can be caused by accepting the
    homage and offerings of Superiors because the receiver's mind
    may be affected.

14 *Animosity*

81. The *bKa' 'gyur* has: 'One is tainted by all wrongs'. Tib: *gos* is
    probably rendered more exactly by 'to clothe' rather than 'to
    taint'.
82. 'Unlike the religious person....' The religious person does the
    opposite of the four things taught in the previous stanza; that
    is, the religious person does not strike back, does not feel
    enmity to those filled with hate, does not return abuse, and
    does not feel animosity even to those who have animosity for
    him or her.
83. The following five stanzas present textual difficulties. *Com.*
    offers two alternative readings. One reading sets up a dispute

between two opposing groups of feuding monks which is then brought to a peaceful conclusion by the words of the reconciler, the Buddha; this has been rejected in this translation in place of the present smoother interpretation.

84. 'Like darkness will never lighten darkness and like smell will never eliminate a smell.'

85. 'The nature of dharma' here refers to a dharma which is always to be practised. Since something dirty, by its nature, cannot remove dirt, this teaching that enmity cannot remove enmity is a statement about the nature of things as they are.

86. When a king who controls a huge empire and exerts great power gains faith in the Buddhist teachings, he abandons everything and goes off alone.

87. 'Matang' is the name of a wilderness; it is suggested that it may be named after a hermit who once lived there.

88. The basic ideas of the immediately preceding verses are elaborated as follows: from one's attachment to getting honours, gifts, food etc., arises bitterness at those better off. This bitterness can lead to intellectual strife, and to the insistence that one's own view is the right view. Seeing the truth of such concepts as four mindfulnesses etc., the correct view which leads to conciliation can be enunciated. Because other teachings lead one astray, one should be wary of those who propound them. It is better to work alone than to associate with such persons, or with any person toward whom one can direct enmity.

15   *Mindfulness*

89. 'Progress' lit. 'the difference between the previous and the latter'. 'The difference' is the resultant understanding of impermanence; 'the previous' is the breathing in, 'the latter' is the breathing out—from which impermanence is realized.

90. 'All of its aspects'. There are four mindfulnesses: of body, mind, feeling, and phenomena.

91. The sentry personifies perseverance, from which all good qualities come.

92. 'Easier', because all good qualities come from perseverance including the nirvana referred to in the previous stanza. 'Fear' refers to fear of misery.

93. The discovery has four aspects: merit, extensive great joy, stabilization and purity. The discovery has merit in that it brings good future life. The extensive great joy and stabilization are a great happiness in this life; purity is the result of the eradication of all contamination.
94. 'Wide awake' refers back to the sentry. Those with perseverance that leads to the results of the Buddhist path are Hearers.
95. The basis of good qualities is refuge in the Three Jewels—Buddha, Doctrine, Community—therefore the Three Jewels are first.
96. Ethics is the basis of a Buddhist's practice.
97. Generosity comes from ethics.
98. From the practice of ethics and generosity the basis for birth in a celestial realm is quickly established and brought to fruition.
99. There are desire realm celestial levels, and form and formless realm celestial levels. This teaches the method to free oneself from birth in the desire realm. See Intro pp.12-14.
100. This teaches the result of meditation on the mindfulness of body—the four stabilizations in the realm of form.
101. This teaches the result of those meditations—mental joy in kindness.
102. This verse points out that one who has calm abiding and has cultivated immeasurable love, compassion etc., could not have malice.
103. This teaches, in general, the cultivation of the meditative stabilization in the form realm.
104. This and the next two verses relate the three doors of liberation (the meditation on emptiness, signlessness and no admiration), to the first three levels of the formless realm. Even these latter meditations are, however, contaminated.
105. 'Nothingness' is the name of the third level of the formless realm.
106. This and the final two verses teach the results of the three doors of liberation.

16 *Miscellaneous*

107. It is after the carefree period of youth and before the onset of old age that religious or meritorious work can be done. Since this period is not permanent, one should utilize it right away.

108. Craving, the cause of rebirth is the 'fault'.
109. This verse was spoken by Buddha to those who mistakenly believed that defilements could be cleansed with water.
110. Without pride, the earlier three are removed.
111. Attachment to outer things.
112. Inner longing desire which brings rebirth, the eighth link in the wheel of life. See Intro p.13-15.
113. This verse explains how it is that a person is said to have or not have the above afflictive emotions. For example, like the wind in a tree rustles all the branches, similarly the sixth consciousness, known as the 'mind' or 'thinking mind' governs and affects the body.
114. Conversely, those without attachment, etc., are the wise.

17   *Water*

115. Buddha, with a group of his monks was received by a benefactor near Magadha. Afterward he crossed the Gaṅgā river with his magical powers. His followers then made their way across. This and the next stanza which describe the event have a deeper meaning. The dam is the path of seeing which leads to the path of meditation by means of which the practitioner goes across to nirvana.
116. 'Are on the dry land' teaches compassion. If he had no compassion a Buddha would not remain.
117. The order of these lines follows *Com.*, which differs slightly from the *bKa' 'gyur*.
118. The learned, free from desire, have no thirst and are like oceans.
119. A doorstep has no anger even when trod underfoot.

18   *The Flower*

120. The first verse is a question directed to Buddha by a god. The second verse is the answer. *Com.* explains that just as the garland maker takes flowers and makes them into garlands which are 'much desired', so too the explanation of Buddha's teaching is in great demand. 'The four things' are the four-part explanation of the teaching of the twelve links, or the four noble truths.

121. Taken literally, 'fears' refers to the danger from wild animals
     and from getting lost, etc. Since such fears do not come from
     one tree but from the forest, it is the forest which is to be
     tackled and cleared away. The deeper meaning is as follows.
     'The forest' is the unbroken, ongoing afflicted mind. 'The tree'
     is gross afflictive emotion. 'Cut' means to make time for
     meditation in that stream of afflicted consciousness. 'Seedlings'
     refers to craving, which gives rise to a stream of afflicted
     consciousness.
122. Non-Buddhist paths take one beyond all the stages of the three
     realms except the last—the peak of existence. This is escaped
     only by cutting the craving which is the bringer of future lives.
123. A queen made a garland for the Buddha. On that occasion he
     taught that one should turn life into a garland of virtues to
     please the Enlightened One and to accomplish one's purpose.
124. Rockhill says this is the *Mimusops elenhi*.
125. Spoken when a licentious king with his many queens picnicked
     on the banks of the Gaṅgā. As they slept, the Gaṅgā rose and
     drowned the women.
126. A body is like a pot, because when dissected, both the pot and
     the body are found to be without a permanent essence.
127. 'Existence' means the aggregates.
128. Foam, being formed in accord with, and lasting only as long as
     the wind, is an example of how one arises from conditions and
     is without a permanent essence.
129. The *udumbara* flower blooms only when a Buddha is on the
     earth.
130. 'What's not beyond' means the aggregates. It is also said that
     the verse refers to the mind which is rid of the superimposition
     of true existence, or a self-sufficient, substantially existent self.
131. The pond is like the mind of the practitioner on the path of
     seeing and meditation. Such a one eliminates afflictions from
     the root.

19 *The Horse*

132. 'Insight' into past lives, etc. It provides the 'mobility', literally
     'legs' of ethics.
133. 'Sense of shame' teaches ethics because shame motivates
     ethical conduct, while lack of shame does not.

134. *Com.* considers three further stanzas, probably the same in their basic outline. The differing couplets are as follows:
   a. For those who properly subdue themselves
      Are liberated from all misery.
      Tib: *sdug bsngal kun las rab grol gyi*
   b. For those who properly subdue themselves
      Eliminate all of the clasps.
      Tib: *kun sbyor ma lus spangs 'gyur gyi*
   c. Those who abide within, properly subdued,
      Are those who have nirvana.
      Tib: *bdag nyid legs 'dul nang gnas pa*
         de ni mya ngan las 'das nyid
   The first of these three verses teaches release from misery in the realm of desire, the second, nirvana with remainder, the last, nirvana with no remainder.
135. 'One's own' means one's mind. When tamed it can lead to nirvana.

20 Wrath

136. 'Conceit' is a name for the root of all afflictive emotions. There are nine 'clasps', corresponding to the nine possible places to take birth (the desire realm is one and there are four levels each in the form and formless realms. See Intro. pp.12-14). Without the clasps there is no future birth and hence no attachments. (See also note 20.)
137. Apply the antidote again and again, at each occurrence of anger or attachment, and thereby cut the clasp which brings rebirth.
138. Tib: *brtul zhugs*, literally: penitent behaviour.
139. This and the following verse are in reverse order in the *Com.*
140. This verse finds its genesis in the story of Maudgalyāyana going by the power of magic to beg from a miser. No matter how much the miser gave, the begging bowl would not fill up.
141. If the horse goes out of control a common trainer cannot even get onto its back to ride. Like an enraged horse gone wild, the ordinary being also becomes completely out of control with wrath.

21 The One Gone Thus

142. Only one universal Buddha, like Śākyamuni who is fourth in a

line of one thousand, can come to this earth at any time. Such a Buddha has achieved the state of omniscience independent of any other Buddha's teachings.

143. Tib: *rgyal ba* means both 'royal' and 'conqueror'.

144. The Buddha immediately preceding Buddha Śākyamuni is held to be the third in the line of the thousand (see note 142 above). The teaching of the third universal Buddha declined until finally no Buddhist teaching remained. Then in that universe devoid of Buddha's word, Śākyamuni arose and turned a new wheel of the doctrine. (See also note 66).

145. This and the next verse refer to the story told at length in the *Singhala Sūtra*. Some traders were stranded in a land of cannibals. The businessman Singhala said to them, 'Remember the King of Horses, (a fabulous horse of the gods in the Heaven of the Thirty-three). When he comes, get on his back and you will be carried back to the world. Otherwise you will be devoured.' The story is a parable for recollection of dharma that carries one to a state of happiness.

146. The two perfect conceptualizations are: the conceptualization of happiness—a state of mind free from all unkindness—and the conceptualization of detachment. The former is named 'of happiness' because it motivates the giving of fearlessness. It is a mind that feels protective towards all. Detachment refers to renunciation. The peace of nirvana results from it. The Buddhas, during their practices, held no conception of an object as desirable. And though all conceptualization are said to be an object of abandonment, these two are taught because they are the cause of accumulating all roots of virtue as well as the cessations.

147. The four hindrances to buddhahood are: craving, dullness, anger and pride; 'quite free' is being free from craving; 'free at heart' is being free from dullness; 'strife' is synonymous with anger; and 'contamination' is with pride and jealousy.

22 *Listening*

148. Line three teaches the path of accumulation. 'To encircle' means to be compatible. When what is to be eliminated is gone, nirvana arises. Line four teaches the path of preparation. 'Religious practice' is the path of seeing. The four divisions of

the path of preparation are compatible with that. This explanation is based on two technical terms, *mthar pa cha mthun* and *nges 'byed cha mthun,* which refer to the path of accumulation and the path of preparation respectively.

149. *Com.* explains these stanzas by means of the example of eyes and a face. Without eyes the face is not complete. Similarly without listening's result, the improved morality which is one's beauty is not complete.

150. There was a superior being whose chanting and voice enthralled king Prasenajit. He was so ugly however, that when Prasenajit took offerings to him, the king felt repulsed; he quickly put down the gifts and left. At that point Buddha said these verses.

151. This and the next four verses are based on the idea that external ephemeral beauty is not a solid basis from which to decide if something is worthy of all one's faith. Buddha is an object of faith. Unshakeable faith in the Buddha, however, is not based on fame or one's intellectual fascination with the Buddha's words and ideas (verse eleven). It is not based on the Buddha's external beauty (verse twelve). Verse thirteen says that without an idea of a Buddha a person cannot have unshakeable faith in him. Verse fourteen presents some textual difficulty. The *bKa' 'gyur* version is probably incorrect. Instead of the *'drang du rung* of the *bKa' 'gyur,* *'drang mi rung* seems more probable. *Com.* seems to favour this phrasing also. (This however, interrupts the flow in the argument. It may, therefore, be better to interpret it as follows: even a wise and renounced being who has any attachment to external beauty, form, or style is in danger of being swayed from belief in the doctrine because of another's beauty or dazzling intellect.)

152. These people are 'patient' because of ethics based on faith and listening; they are 'befriended by joy' because of being content, with few desires.

23 *Self*

153. The first two lines teach the accumulation of wisdom and merit respectively. The last two lines teach the result: physical and mental detachment.

154. One first eliminated all afflictive emotion within oneself. Whatever is to be taught is first to be actualized by oneself.
155. One's own work of mind training becomes a branch of working for others.
156. This and the next verse teach the benefits that accrue in this life.
157. This and the next verse teach the benefits that come in the next life.
158. The object of abandonment of the path of seeing.
159. The benefit of the path of seeing.
160. The benefit of the path of meditation.
161. The path of no more learning, because a master is somebody who is of benefit.
162. Nirvana without remainder. Tradition has two different audiences to which the Buddha said these words. The first is a group of fourteen itinerant religious beings; the second is a sick and grumpy abbot who was neglected by his disciples.

24 *Comparisons*

163. Buddha spoke this verse to a brahmin who began a lengthy recitation of the Vedas.
164. This refers to the path of seeing.
165. The attainment of the fourth concentration. Here all physical and mental happiness is removed and there is only equanimity.
166. Nirvana with remainder.
167. Nirvana without remainder; 'immutable' because a permanent functioning thing.
168. The state is difficult to 'see' because it is not an object of sense consciousness.
169. The 'holy state' is the object of all Superiors.
170. The 'immortal state' is the one of no degeneration.
171. The 'nectarous state' is undying.
172. 'Dust' means afflictive emotions.
173. 'Dust-free state' is the absence of any objects giving rise to afflictive emotions. These verses, highly repetitive in structure, refute wrong ideas of nirvana held by non-Buddhists.
174. An ascetic practice of making fire offerings and eating only a few seeds each month.

175. The wisdom of the realization that reality is the root of compassion and kindness. Dharma here means this realization.

25   Intimate Friends

176. 'Who speak gently' is explained as having appropriate shame, awareness, and appropriate embarrassment.
177. 'Things', literally grounds. These grounds are the causes of virtue and non-virtue, etc. Hearing and pondering are the causes for faith and wisdom.
178. The student will be imbued with the good and bad qualities of the teacher, just as that which is wrapped by anything is stained by its wrapper.
179. A spoon is in the pot for years but the taste of what is cooking never rubs off on it.
180. A king, from hearing a single line of commentary, understood the four truths, while Devadatta, who was a monk and could recite by heart all scriptures, took birth in hell.

26   Nirvana

181. 'Contracts conceptual thought' teaches mental detachment. There are four disturbing conceptual states of mind or thoughts: afflictive emotions, non-afflictive emotions, the taste of stabilization and scorn for the path. Only nirvana without remainder is free from all four. 'Not relying' on family etc., teaches physical detachment.
182. The second verse carries on the meaning of 'nor doing others harm'. There are three patiences: the one toward harmful beings, the one to miseries like heat and cold, and the one toward the difficult meditation on selflessness. Line one teaches the first two, and line two teaches the third patience through which nirvana is achieved.
183. Because it cannot be cured as long as one has a body.
184. A 'range' is where the various beings live or where they go when there is danger. 'Intellect' means the faculty of analysis and making choices. The *bKa' 'gyur* has *bsgoms,* 'meditation' instead of *Com., shes rab,* 'intelligence'.
185. There are two basic ways to look at the twelve links: from the point of view of their progressive unfolding, and from the

point of view of their removal. In this and the next five stanzas, nirvana is taught by explaining the removal of misery and its origin.

186. The first two lines teach the four noble truths and the worldly understanding that realizes them. The third line teaches the trans-worldly or transcendent understanding of the four truths. It is by realizing what is 'hard to see'—the truth of misery together with its cause which has been bringing the bad result—that cessation together with the path is attained. (The first three lines, begining with 'hard to see', can be interpreted also as a method of developing the intelligence by means of hearing, thinking and meditation, and non-contaminated understanding.) Through such intelligence nirvana is attained.

187. This verse teaches removal of attachment in each of the three realms. The last example is explained in *Com.* as follows: Just as a long river flows from a lake, the lifespan is very long in the formless realm.

188. Each of the next four stanzas convey the same meaning. They teach the removal of misery and its origin (the first two truths), and cessation and the path to cessation. Buddha taught the verses to different kings in this and in the realm of the gods.

189. When ordinary beings look on a beautiful body, the beauty they perceive is present only because they are looking with attachment; the wealth they think they amass by doing various deeds is only by hearsay, not actually definite; the objects of sense-consciousness are 'perceived' merely because of conditions; and one's idea of experiencing pleasure is actually just the function of consciousness. When such mental attachments are abandoned there is peace.

190. This verse is said to be easily comprehensible to a certain type of god, to whom Buddha taught it. ('This' refers to the suffering body; 'mother' refers to its cause. 'Pain' refers to the cessation of pain, and 'great pain' refers to the path.)

191. This verse is also related to the four truths. 'No hope' means true misery, 'no loves', the true origin, etc.

192. This is the twelve links from the point of view of their progressive unfolding. It is the explanation of the process through which one comes to enter and abide in cyclic existence. See also Intro. pp.13-15.

193. 'Strife' means miseries from environment such as cold, insect bites, and the like.

194. This is the twelve links from the point of view of their progressive removal.
195. 'Composites' refer to uncontaminated primordial wisdom.
196. The four sources are names for the four divisions of the formless realm.
197. 'Brahmin Conqueror' means a Foe Destroyer. 'Brahmin' refers to the achieving of a state where another body is not taken: 'Conqueror' refers to having overcome all afflictive emotions.
198. 'What is comparable' means the aggregate of form—which is the same before and after the mind achieves nirvana. 'What is not comparable' means the mind in nirvana, which is also left behind at death. 'Composites' here means all other births and their attendant misery.

27 *Seeing*

199. This fault-finding defiles or obscures pure view.
201. Shamelessness is the cause of not seeing reality.
202. The 'cycle of darkness' is the cycle of existence; the reason a being is trapped in this cycle is ignorance.
203. The explanation of the selflessness of persons that follows is difficult. 'Other stuff' means the self; it is adhered to as being substantially different from the aggregates. This is known as the adherence to a self of persons.
204. Two non-Buddhist views are referred to here. The first is that one is oneself such a creator. The second is that a permanent and partless creator like Brahmā created people. There are many such views, all of which, according to the Buddhist view, obscure the correct understanding of selflessness, without which liberation cannot be gained.
205. 'Sharp pain' is the adherence to the notions 'self' and 'mine'.
206. 'Craving object' means adherence to a false sense of self.
207. The first two lines refer to adherence to self in each of the three realms. The 'disputatious people' are holders of the sixty-two wrong views of self. Arguing among themselves, they never find liberation.
208. 'Covered by dust' means covered by the sorrows of life, the pervading misery of cyclic existence. 'All that has been achieved', etc. means the aggregates of this and future lives.
209. 'Make an essence' means that while having adherence to self and mine, one believes good deeds are a cause of liberation.

210. The result (second instant) of such a path of insight is liberation.

211. The first of the four mindfulnesses is mindfulness of body.

212. The royal chariot is in fact plain wood, but colourfully decorated, it seems beautiful and catches the eye. So too the unclean body, when painted and ornamented, is the object of the common person's desire.

213. The 'best' unattached being has no clasping to upper realms. The 'final' being has no clasping to the desire realm. The 'fully' unattached being has no clasping to all three realms. All the clasps are eliminated through the paths of seeing and meditation.

214. Just renouncing one's home is not alone a sufficient method to eliminate clasps. This verse was spoken by Buddha in disapproval of a man who hated home life and took to the woods. After a while the man reverted to his old home life and then, growing unhappy, again went off and became a hermit. The deeper meaning is as follows. 'The thicket' is one's body; 'the woods' stands for the turbulent mind of the householder. Both the body and mind should be made free of troublesome things in the forest retreat where liberation is gained.

215. The Buddha spoke this verse when a queen, interested in Buddha's doctrine, travelled toward him in her chariot. On the deeper level it teaches that liberation is gained through the eightfold path. Right speech, boundary of action, and livelihood are said to be included in ethics. 'White canopy' refers to right understanding and liberation, purified of afflictions of the three realms. 'Matching spokes' refers to right remembrance, realization and stabilization. 'Having' the spokes refers to right effort; the 'carriage' itself refers to right belief. The liberation and understanding exemplified by the white canopy comprise the eightfold path itself.

216. 'Refuge' means to rely on an object to eliminate the wrongs one has earlier done.

217. These three compose the Triple Gem.

218. The sense of 'refuge' here encompasses faith and understanding which are also needed to obtain liberation. Faith and understanding come from the realization of the four truths by non-contaminated wisdom.

219. The final five verses may have various interpretations. *Com.* is itself somewhat obscure. However, the basic distinction is

between 'seeing'—the direct non-conceptual understanding of the selflessness of persons, and 'simulated' or 'affected seeing'—the seeing done by ordinary beings who take their bodies and belongings to be possessions of a substantially self-sufficient person. Besides this, *Com.* also indicates a twofold aspect to the non-conceptual realization of the four truths; the new seeing of the nature of the body etc., and the seeing of something again beyond that—the cessation of misery and liberation.

28 *Evil*

220. Line one teaches the way to perfect all virtue. Line two teaches the result of pure ethics. These two are the cause of the result taught in line three, and that result itself is the cause of the nirvana of line four.
221. Buddha saw a new-born child who cried until it saw a monk; this showed that the wise want only to be with good spiritual friends.
222. 'Peace and complete detachment' are synonyms here for abiding and insight. 'The taste of liking dharma' is nirvana.
223. 'Virtue and evil' refer to the two upper realms and the realm of desire respectively. 'Mental contamination' is the dripping of mind to the objects of the senses. *Com.* has *bcom*, 'overcome' instead of the *bKa' 'gyur, bcos*, 'warp'.
224. This verse emphasizes that it is not austerities, but reliance on pure conduct that brings liberation.
225. This and the following two verses are the answer of Buddha to Anāthapiṇḍada, the great benefactor, who asked about the habituation of the mind to good and bad.
226. As, for example, Devadatta's unbearable headache after he heaved a rock at Buddha.
227. 'Anguish' can be thought of as the fruition of evil in this and future lives, while the 'sorrow' two verses later is the intense regret which arises when the realization dawns of the coming misery. The distinction between the two is also between the former as mental and the latter as physical pain. 'Intense anguish' encompasses not only simple daily anguish and sorrow, but the anguish and sorrow which arise from having to remain among enemies and cut off from friends.

228. A 'pure deed' is recognized because it is one which brings about a pleasurable result.
229. *Com.* makes no comment on 'white deeds' except to relate the passage to the story of Queen Somanāsā who, through virtue, took birth in a celestial realm. 'White deeds' bring a happy migration.
230. A religious or Dharmic person is explained, at this point, to be someone who has compassion and intelligence. The final two verses comprise the answer of the future Buddha Śākyamuni to the demons who surrounded him as he sat beneath the bodhi tree. They asked 'Are you not afraid?' and he responded as given in the text.
231. 'Taught' means that Śākyamuni, the fourth universal Buddha, followed the teaching of the earlier Buddha in previous lives, and accumulated merit and wisdom on the path of accumulation, etc.

29   Antitheses

232. The last two verses in the preceding set were spoken just before the attainment of enlightenment, while sitting beneath the bodhi tree. This set of verses continues from that point, describing the light of teaching of the universal Buddha. 'Philosophers' are propounders of the doctrine of self.
233. 'What is likeable' is fourfold: discourse, view, stabilization, and liberation. They follow one from the other. 'What is not likeable' is cyclic existence.
234. 'Misconceived' in the sense of a practice that does not lead to liberation. Thus it is also the belief in a self.
235. *Com.* gives many interpretations of this verse. 'Beliefs' are in self, etc. 'What has been heard' means fruitless, extreme austerities. 'Making anew and increasing' means going through the twelve links.
236. 'Striving' means the initial antidote, 'good work' leads to the actual antidote, and 'cogitation' is the actual antidote, i.e. the path of seeing, the direct non-conceptual realization itself. What is 'experienced' and 'doubts' are the abandonments of the path of seeing.
237. 'First rank' means a naturally virtuous person.
238. When the topmost bud of the palmyra tree is cut it withers and dies.

239. Tib: *dgon pa,* is a place a half mile or more from a town. It is also the Tibetan word for monastery.

240. 'Truth' means suchness or selflessness.

241. Tib: *so sor rtogs pa,* 'analytic realization'. With this realization even gross provocation such as the one taught in the next verse does not upset one.

242. A verse seems to be missing from the *bKa' 'gyur* at this point. Reconstructing it from *Com.* it should read:

I have seen fearful cyclic existence
And its recurrence.
Therefore I have no liking of existence.
(See also Rockhill page 145, note 2.)

243. The next two verses describe a holy being or a being without any attachment to the world. In the country Katsagala lived a monk called Ratna. He had the six extrasensory perceptions, but became sick with a terrible mange and a palsy of the arms and legs. To keep others from losing faith by seeing his physical disabilities, and by seeing that he did not make prostrations and other forms of obeisance, he lived alone, going from forest to forest, from deserted house to deserted house. He did not even visit a village to beg. This verse is applicable to him.

The deeper meaning is as follows. 'No faith' means no liking for cyclic existence; 'unmade' is nirvana; 'pay back' means to realize; 'human' means one without attachment; 'home' means what brings future birth (i.e. afflictive emotion); 'pierce' means abandon; 'destroy chance' means to eliminate future migration; to 'eat vomit' is to be free of craving.

244. In a mountainous country a warrior who wanted to be king killed his parents, the king and others, and seized the throne. The Buddha knew that this king would be shattered by any direct teaching. Therefore the Buddha taught him through this verse, and in consequence, the king became a great benefactor and acquired merit.

The deeper meaning is in terms of the twelve links. There are two interpretations. 'Mother' means craving, 'father' is contaminated actions and existence (the second and tenth links respectively in the wheel of life). 'King' means consciousness, 'two saints' means holding wrong view as best and holding bad ethics and behaviour as best, 'country' means objects of afflicted mind and 'retinue' is the twenty close afflictions.

When all these are eliminated by the antidote there is purity.

The second interpretation takes 'mother' as unknowing (the first link in the wheel of life), 'father' as composite action (the second link), 'king' as consciousness, ('the king arises by the condition of the father'), 'the two saints' as name and form, 'people' as the six sources, (the objects of the king-consciousness) and the 'retinue' as contact, feeling and the other mental factors found with the king-consciousness. When these are eliminated then craving, attachment, etc., are purified.

245. Buddha said these verses with the monk Kauṇḍinya in mind. Once Buddha was living in a rocky retreat place. At that time the monk entered nirvana beneath a tree near a cow path. Two cowgirls came across his body and recognized it as that of the monk to whom they had often given alms. They therefore offered their vessels of milk to the body. They took his begging bowl and robes to give to the monks and used the tree to cremate him. Four golden-coloured apparitional birds appeared in the sky at that time.

'Amass nothing' means to take no rebirth. 'Know' refers to the knowledge of what is to be abandoned and of the non-conceptual. There are four types of food. Knowing them all implies being free of attainment in all three spheres. 'Migration' is birth itself, 'footprints' are the result of migration or birth. For one in nirvana there is neither. The last two lines teach the path to liberation called the three doors of liberation. They are the means by which the result taught in the first two lines is attained.

246. Prajñāvarman, in an effort to find meaning in the repetition, remarks that the same medicine will be administered time and time again throughout the duration of a sickness. He also conjectures that Buddha may have repeated verses for late comers and praises Buddha's insight into the needs of his disciples.

247. 'Dharma' means hearing, considering and cultivating the teaching received from a spiritual friend. It is the practice of the path from which arises insight into the four truths.

248. The great benefactor Anāthapiṇḍada was cured of a fever just by seeing the face of the Buddha. He then inquired as to where

his pain had gone. 'Beyond time' means beyond birth. 'Protector' means without attachment to form and therefore the protector of one's own happiness. 'Knots' are attachments to the formless realm.

249. The 'precipice' leads to bad migrations. 'Clasps and knots' are objects of abandonment of the paths of seeing and meditation respectively. 'He', on this occasion, refers to a monk who achieved nirvana in a forest retreat.

250. The sun can dry an ordinary swamp and set free the animals trapped there, but nothing external or physical can touch the swamp of desire.

251. The *bKa' 'gyur* has *srid pa*, 'existence'.

252. 'Religious being' means a Superior, one with non-conceptual realization of selflessness.

253. 'Elaboration' indicates those objects of cyclic existence which encourage the mind to become scattered or diffused. 'Infant' is one who cannot differentiate cyclic existence and nirvana. One Gone Thus; Skt: *Tathāgata: tathā* is suchness, and *gata* is gone, here meaning to understand. (See also compilation of verses about the One Gone Thus.)

254. There are four types of clasps; Tib: *kun sbyor:* desire, existence, belief and ignorance. All are afflictions that hold one to the three realms. From them come the other afflicted minds of liking existence, hating enemies, etc. Clasps, which are deeply ingrained in the fabric of the minds of infants, are loosened by seeing selflessness. (See also notes 20 and 136).

255. Although in general 'existence' means cyclic existence, here it is the term for the tenth link in the wheel of life. Its use is a case of the word that describes the result being applied to the cause. It is the mental force (karma) immediately previous to the taking of a new rebirth.

256. The *bKa' 'gyur* has *smros shig. Com.,* which has *slod shig,* says this is a discourse at once logical and in accord with the scriptures.

257. The 'seer' is Buddha, his 'ensign' is the flag by which his presence is known and 'eloquence' is a discourse from which realization occurs effortlessly. It is the possession of the Foe Destroyer alone; it conveys special meaning and benefits others.

258. In the *Com.* the later line 'Though they walk forth', is inserted here. Since it interrupts the flow of thought, the *bKa' 'gyur* has been retained.

259. 'Flawless' indicates caution and effort because these two are the cause of uninterrupted virtue.

260. 'Roots' are the basic adherence to self; 'leaves' are pride thinking 'I', 'stalks' are craving. The first is the root of all that is bad. The second stands up like a huge, leafy tree. The third exemplifies craving because even in a strong rock house, stalks of weeds push up and grow.

261. Desire and the five objects of the senses are 'base elaboration'. The 'sorrowful clasp' is anger.

262. 'Unmoving' means to future migration.

263. Line one teaches the emergence from the realm of desire into the first concentration where one has no experience of external objects of the senses. Line two teaches the emergence from the first into the second concentration where one experiences neither rough nor subtle conceptualization. 'All clasps', (the craving for joy and the craving for happiness), are what must be abandoned to emerge into the third and fourth concentrations. When 'forms and discriminations' are abandoned one leaves the realm of form. 'The four yogas' are the four formless realms.

30 *Happiness*

264. A Nihilist Brahmin tried to goad Buddha by calling him 'Conqueror' over and over again. Buddha answered him with this verse.

265. Religion and irreligion are what benefits and hurts other beings respectively.

266. A rich merchant with faith in Buddha went to his own storeroom to select a cloth to give as an offering. All the cloth looked so beautiful to him that he could not bring himself to give any away. The verse was prompted by this incident.

267. This verse explains how giving and battle are similar in terms of being a cause.

268. This verse shows that in general giving is better than war.

269. 'Other' would be, for example, diseases, etc.

270. 'By insight' refers to cultivating the deep understanding of the direct realization of the four truths. Tib: *reg ga*, 'gained', (literally, touched).

271. This is the 'faith' in the doctrine of the four truths which develops after having realization of them.

272. 'What is not born' is nirvana.

273. 'The seven branches' refer to the path of seeing. The four limbs are usually associated with the path of accumulaltion. Here, however, they refer to the path of meditation.

274. Because nirvana is achieved through the eightfold path, it refers to the path of no more learning.

275. 'Eat in happiness' means without incurring a debt for what is eaten.

276. 'Pride in self' is the innate view that looks on the aggregates and mistakenly adheres to a self which exists as substantially as those aggregates seem to do.

277. 'Adhere' means to serve and honour. Mother and father benefit oneself. Brahmins (i.e. householders) and ordained beings (i.e. monks and nuns) possess estimable qualities.

278. 'In accord' means working in accord with the teachings; 'according austerities' is the elimination of afflictive emotions as taught by Buddha.

279. Ethics, hearing much, and liberation are achieved by removing the inner and outer stains. The outer stains are removed by the river, the inner by relying on the holy beings.

280. 'Happy course' carries the idea of smooth banks, and water running easily. There people wash, drink, water fields, etc.

281. Tib: *cang shes*, 'thoroughbred' is a type of miraculous animal.

282. They have the great qualities of mind whether born in the family of a king or a slave. In that state they progress from purity to purity, to greater and greater happiness.

283. 'Infection' means a coarse afflictive emotion like anger which immediately disturbs peace of mind.

284. Taking a new set of aggregates when reborn.

285. *Com.* gives another, clearer example. Water courses with different designations flow down into one bigger river and hence into the sea where they are indistinguishable and have no different names. Similarly beings have different names until they are in the state of nirvana. The change from our present state to nirvana is like the movement of redness in molten iron.

After the iron has cooled one cannot point to where the redness has gone.

286. *Com.* has *srid pa,* 'existence' and *srid min,* 'no-existence' (which refer to the desire realm and the upper realms respectively) for *sred pa,* 'craving' and *sred min,* 'non-craving'.

287. All sentient beings have aggregates and the attendant misery. These arise from the related causes and conditions and one is under the power of them.

288. A monk achieved nirvana in the early hours of the morning and sang out 'Ah! I am happy.' When asked why, he spoke this and the following verse which he said the Buddha had recited earlier.

289. 'Sickness' is anger.

290. To teach that hurting others arises from attachment and anger.

291. A king gave up his attachment to the kingdom of Mithilā. When it caught fire Buddha spoke these words to him.

292. 'God of Clear Light'. There are three heavens in the second concentration of the form realm. One of the heavens is called the Clear Light Heaven. There the gods sustain themselves with the ecstasy of their mental stabilization.

293. The Buddha can sustain himself with such food because he is not attached to any object of the world.

294. According to the teaching of the twelve links. Tib: *len pa,* 'attachment', is said to arise from craving.

295. 'Everywhere' means that no matter what type of people one meets, their kindness or nastiness does not cause like or dislike and a corresponding happiness or depression.

31   *The Mind*

296. 'Light' means easily moved, going from place to place like a monkey in the tree. 'Hard to grasp' because even great disciples like Ānanda found it hard to know just exactly what mind is.

297. 'The base of demons' is the actual afflictive emotions. 'Base' can also be used in the sense of 'content' or 'meaning'.

298. This verse stresses that the mind can be tamed. But in order to tame it one must have skill.

299. Mind is 'unseen' by sense consciousness, and 'essenceless' because it is impermanent, lasting only an instant.

300. 'In the right way' means by cultivating the antidotes to afflictive emotions.

301. 'The house-builder' is the state of mind defined as directing or willing the taking of a new set of aggregates. 'Beams' stand for ignorance, 'frames' stand for craving; 'the end' means that in this life the mind reposes in nirvana.

302. This reading follows *Com., sems ni g. yo zhing yang ba ste*. The *bKa' 'gyur* has *sems ni g. yo zhing rdzun pa ste*, 'mind is deceitful, a dissembler'. It is 'fickle' because it is a motivator of different karma. 'Travel off' means it is hard to make it be virtuous, and it is 'hard to stop' from going into wrong paths.

303. Proper meditation is like the hot fire used to melt the kinks out of a previously crooked mind. The bent nature of the mind is almost structural. If one tries to merely pull it into a new form it reverts to its old nature. But when the fire of meditation is used to dissolve the kinks and make a new straight form, the new shape will remain.

304. 'Goes far' refers to the thinking mind—other sense consciousnesses being more limited in range. It 'travels alone' because each person's continuum is an entity separate from other beings. 'Dwelling within' relates the consciousness to feeling, the sixth link in the wheel of life, but this is not a consciousness that can be subdued just by withdrawing external stimuli. The point is that Buddha's method for liberation consists of dealing with the inner mind. It is not just the simple withdrawal of stimuli.

305. Tib: *bsgoms*, 'habituated', 'cultivated' or 'meditated'. The mind must be continually familiarized with the virtuous path until the smallest chink through which afflictive emotion exerts influence is blocked. Such a cultivated mind is known as equipoise and is untainted by any afflictive emotions.

306. The second line answers possible objections to line one. 'Principal' answers the objection that mental factors such as feeling associated with thinking-mind motivate actions. 'Swift' is understood when the principal mind and mental factors are compared to a king and his retinue. The king's orders are immediately carried out by the retinue. A more simple explanation of the passage would be that it is the relation of mind to body and speech.

307. A son of a Brahmin and a prince were listening to the Buddha

preach. He said, 'First eat, then give the remainder to others.' Because of the particular circumstances, the former became incensed by this teaching while the latter generated a deep faith. On account of his attitude the former's head was severed by a wheel as he lay sleeping beneath a tree near the road, while the latter was sponsored by a wealthy merchant who noticed that the shade of a tree fell on the prince even when the position of the sun required it to fall in a different direction.

308. Perfecting oneself depends on receiving eloquent or well-spoken teachings. However, people with agitated minds cannot hear or take in such eloquence.

309. Candra-śri, a heartless criminal, undertook a contract to kill Buddha. Waiting for him among the disciples on the steps of Vulture Peak, three times he called out from his place asking Buddha to speak. Buddha spoke these lines and the criminal was moved, became a monk and achieved nirvana.

310. Prince Sumukha asked the Buddha, 'Whose fame declines?' This verse comprises the answer. *Com.* refers to the thirty-six afflictive emotions in the realm of desire. The metaphor seems to work with the idea of contamination: the dripping or flowing out to objects of desire.

311. 'Coarse sensibilities' are the cause of coarse pleasures. 'Feeble power of mind' is torpor brought on by satiation.

312. 'Time to rise' means time to do virtuous deeds.

313. 'Strong'; *Com.* relates this word to the five endowments bestowed by others.

314. Tib: *g. yen spyo*, 'search out fault'. Scattered mind is brought on by this. 'Trifling' refers to the object of desire, 'tiny' to the small misconceptions in the mind when in deep meditation.

315. 'Skill in conceptions' means to know which ideas are valid and which are not. 'Each' means each stage of equipoise; 'every' means including the latencies.

316. A pot is caused, it will break, and it is filled with fluids. A city is full of people of all different castes and occupations surrounded by a fence of bones.

317. 'Transient' refers to the five aggregates in general.

318. The *bKa' 'gyur* has *de bzhin chos rnams smig rgyu 'dra shes nas*, 'And seeing phenomena as a mirage'. This follows *Com.*

319. 'The exclusive place' is nirvana, because it gives no ground to afflictive emotions and is not a ground on which further cyclic existence comes into being.

320. Tired of the incessant quarrelling among the community in Vaishali, Buddha flew up into the sky. He saw an old tusker, sick of leading a herd of fighting bull-elephants, go off alone. The verse was spoken on that occasion. Line one describes the mind of the One Gone Thus and line two describes a large elephant. Line three, in the *sNar thang* edition is *sems dang sems mi mnyams pas na,* this is changed to the *sDer dge* edition's *ni mnyams pas na,* 'because they are alike'. The first mind seems to refer to the mind of the elephant, and its wish to avoid combat. It seems better, however, to relate it to the actual elephant itself.

321. 'Love' is a compassionate mind wanting all sentient beings to be free of misery. 'Affection' is a mind wanting them all to be happy. To be without 'malicious thoughts' is to cultivate joy in others' happiness.

322. The last line may be interpreted as teaching the fourth boundless meditation, of equanimity; alternatively it may be understood as the result of the previous three.

323. 'Doctrine of virtue' is ethics and stabilization which are the basis of special insight.

324. 'Right understanding' is special or heightened insight united with calm abiding or meditative stabilization.

325. The queens of Ajātaśatru and their retinue were sporting close to Vultures Peak. The populace of Rajgir were ohing-and-ahing at the pleasure they were having. Buddha spoke these verses to the monks at that time.

326. Spoken to Ānanda as he grieved over the death of Sundarika.

327. Tib: *kyob,* 'saviour': those with a stability of mind that does not waver.

328. 'Mighty' are those on the path of no more learning.

329. A couple of demons were fighting near to the place where Śāriputra was meditating. They disturbed his *samādhi*. He told them to be quiet, and was quite unhappy when, in retaliation, they struck him on the head with a sword. Buddha spoke this verse on that occasion.

330. The stages in calming the mind; this was spoken at Śrārvastī when some monks became upset over the putrid corpse of a dog left by the side of the road. 'Find fault'—literally, say of something that exists, that it does not. 'Yoga of exalted mind' is the practice of the four concentrations. 'Personal liberation vows' are *pratimoksa* vows.

331. 'Mental signs': knowing the divisions of consciousness into sense consciousness etc., and knowing which aspects of mind take objects to be desirable. Knowing what is afflictive emotion and what is bare consciousness. 'Intent' is calm abiding.

332. 'Perverse views' are abandoned on the path of seeing, 'sleep and fog' are abandonments on the path of meditation and 'the demon' is afflictive emotions.

333. 'Right conception' is renunciation.

334. Rebirth in one of these lower realms—hells, animal or hungry ghost—depends on whether the misdeed is strong, middling or weak.

32 The Monk

335. A monk arose from a week-long deep absorption in meditation and went to beg food. One of the gods saw him and manifested as a rich householder, and told him to come to eat. 'No,' said the monk, 'I will go to a poorer place.' The god then manifested as a carpet weaver and told his wife to give the monk food. She heaped good food in his bowl. 'Sister,' said the monk, 'please do not give me so much and such good food again.' Thereon all the gods rejoiced. 'Another' can refer either to other persons related to the monk in this life, or it can refer to another future life. 'Refuge', because the monk teaches and benefits others.

336. The 'dust' is longing desire. To 'clear the dust that lies before' is to clean longing desire from one's mental continuum. To 'not need to chat with others' means that one doesn't need to talk with or impress others to try to obtain food. The entire verse is used to teach pure and impure livelihood. The impetus for it is Shariputra going to eat at the house of a relative and while there, teaching the doctrine to the others gathered for the meal. A Brahmin who was present became angry and said, 'Misled himself, he goes around misleading others.'

337. A 'well-placed' mind is one which is governed by wisdom and compassion.

338. 'By trade' lit. 'by making things'.

339. On the path of seeing and then on the path of meditation the practitioner first observes objects of the desire realm and eliminates the afflictive emotion directly related with them.

Through this, the afflictions found only in the state of equipoise are eliminated. In this way the practitioner 'works alone'. 'Selfless' refers to the path of seeing; 'free of craving' refers to the path of meditation, the antidote to 'desire and craving'.

340. Even though not rich, one is exhorted to 'share' by giving teachings and other material things to others.

341. This verse enumerates 'the forms of conduct' of the verses just above. This provides a general description of the complete monk or nun.

342. Those who do as described in the first three lines 'do not fall completely from' the wisdom of hearing, thinking about and meditating on doctrine.

343. To 'see well' means to realize the four truths.

344. 'Happiness' is mental bliss; 'joy' is the end of the task.

345. The many happinesses are antidotes which are applied higher and higher on the path to liberation.

346. The monk Maudgalyāyana had been severely beaten by Guḍaśikhiyaka. Some Brahmins and householders asked whether he had been upset by the beating. This verse and the next five were given in reply to their question.

347. This verse may be read as describing either one true or complete monk who has all three qualities, or as describing three types of monks, one for each line.

348. This was spoken to refute wrong ideas of what constitutes a monk.

349. Tib: *sde tshogs*, 'society'—any faults in following the path of a Superior. When such faults have been given up, then all of one's time is given over to being of benefit to others.

350. This and the next five verses are said to have been spoken as Buddha and his disciples were approaching the river Gaṅgā. The ferrymen shouted and abused them from afar, but as they approached, the wonderful calm emanating from them caused the ferrymen to say gently and with respect, 'Please give me the houour of having you in my boat.'

351. Tib: *lta bas mi ngoms*, means to not be satisfied by seeing. This last line therefore may refer to the objects of the world and the changeable misery that arises due to them. Though at first such objects give rise to a feeling of pleasure the feeling soon turns to discomfort. Thus that type of 'seeing' does not give lasting satisfaction.

352. Tib: *sdu byed,* 'composites' means a seed or volition capable of giving rise to something. Subduing the aggregates gives release from taking aggregates, i.e. rebirth, again.

353. 'Shakes out' is the action of eliminating all objects of afflictive emotion in the realm of desire.

354. A monk asked Buddha this question: 'Buddha, you say "A monk is one in constant peace". How does a monk become that way?'

355. Generally, when talking about the meditation of stabilization combined with special insight, the stabilization called calm abiding must be achieved first. That special insight develops from the established calm abiding. When the meditation of stabilization combined with the special insight is actually achieved, the merits amassed on the path of accumulation have become sufficient to gain the prize. The person is then said to be on the path of preparation. On the path of preparation the practitioner does much meditation in preparation for the non-conceptual direct realization. The attainment of this direct realization is also called the attainment of the path of seeing.

356. See note 330.

357. 'Aspect', literally, dharma, is the wisdom cultivating the seven factors of enlightenment. Buddha said a monk was 'a being in equipoise'.

358. The word 'personal' points to the true origin of the ordinary beings: adherence to self. 'Here' means in this life. 'Uncontaminated One' means Foe Destroyer.

359. 'Ethics' is guarding against those acts which are naturally non-virtuous, such as the act of killing; 'conduct' is the guarding against those acts which have been stipulated as non-virtuous, such as drinking alcohol or eating in the evening.

360. Tib: *gdeng drod chod.* The meaning of this phrase is obscure. The translation here is based on a suggestion by Palden Drakpa, librarian of Tibet House, New Delhi.

361. The aggregates appear to be, either individually or as a whole, a unit unto themselves, and to have the qualities of being permanent, pleasant and clean. The person holding the self to be 'an aggregate', in the sense of 'as substantial as an aggregate' is miserable; (this is the wrong view of the transient collection according to some Vaibhāṣikas.) When one sees that the aggregates are impermanent, in the nature of misery, and unclean,

and when one cannot discover the self as previously conceived, then one finds liberation.

362. This nonconceptual understanding of selflessness is the dividing line between ordinary beings and Superiors.

363. 'Who become different' means who take rebirth; 'attached to' means liking for outer things; 'like' means enjoying the experiences; 'pronounced attachment' is to have thorough enjoyment. Worldly beings 'look on and like' this life and future life. The focus of the last two lines of this verse shifts away from the desire realm. 'That which they like' is the formless realm, mistakenly believed to be liberation and 'that which they fear' is selflessness, the realization of which is the means to nirvana.

364. A Brahmin and religious person are synonymous here. 'Renounced' means that one is at the end of cyclic existence.

365. The twelve links in the wheel of dependent origination can be divided into three thoroughly afflicted groups: the first group, comprised of the second and tenth links, is called thoroughly afflicted karma; the second group, comprised of the first, fifth and ninth links is called thoroughly afflictive emotions; the third group, comprised of the remaining seven links is called thoroughly afflicted arisings. These three groups go round continually, giving rise to each other. Tib: *len pa*, 'taking' (the name for the ninth link) usually translated, 'attachment', is understood primarily as a name for the true origin, the first two of the above thoroughly afflicted groups. Here, however, it is a general name for the thoroughly afflicted.

366. This verse explains how 'taking' is removed.

367. [time] i.e. death.

368. The demon of the afflictive emotions. Line two teaches calm body, speech and mind.

369. 'The swamp' is made of the desires which hold one; 'thorns of the town' are offerings and services and homage one is given.

370. 'beyond' Tib: *rjes thob*, literally 'subsequent attainment'.

371. See note 158.

372. Poison spreads throughout the body; the medicine cures all snake bites.

373. The monks built a dam at Śrāvastī so that they could cross to beg and return with their food. The repetition is said to be on account of seven people who wanted to be monks. They came to Buddha, and since each person was afflicted by one emotion

more strongly than another, this and the next six verses were said.

374. The pain of doubt is an abandonment of the path of seeing.

375. All coarse and subtle conceptualizations are eliminated in meditation on the first concentration. In the higher concentrations and formless realm there is no conceptualization.

376. *Com.* adds a line here not found in the *bKa' 'gyur:* Tib. *kun gzhi 'ga' med,* ('the monks without any basis for all').

377. 'Jungle' means craving.

378. 'Contagious disease' is anger which gives pain both at the time and later.

379. The last two verses sum up the qualities of the monk explained earlier. A god inquired of Buddha, 'Who is a monk? Who is one in concentration? Who is a yogi? Who is in ecstasy?' Tib: *bsam gtan,* 'concentration'; in general there are four concentrations but in this instance it refers to the seeing of reality in a state of equipoise. Yogis who 'do that work' are those in unbroken concentration.

380. The last verse summarizes the qualities of the complete monk. It explains the four aspects of one of a noble lineage: embracing what is to be done and abandoning what is to be rejected, being content with just robes, just meagre food and just a poor place to sleep.

33 *The Brahmin*

381. The verse can be understood as a description of the progressive development as a person goes along the path to nirvana. It can also be read so that each line can be taken as definition of each of the three types of beings.

382. The *bKa' 'gyur* has *rdzab,* 'mud' instead of *Com. bregs,* 'baldness'. Both readings are possible, being external methods by which liberation is sought.

383. 'Uncertainty' is eliminated by the path of seeing.

384. Literally 'intermediate state' between birth and death. Here it refers to cyclic existence in general.

385. Tib: *nyid,* 'selves'. The word is to point out the fact that they have not realized selflessness.

386. Feeling gives rise to craving, the eighth link in the wheel of life. By removing feeling, craving is eliminated.

387. Feelings which are caused by extreme views cause attachment to the three realms.

388. A caste-Brahmin was living beside the Balgumata river misleading the populace with his outward appearance. When Buddha spoke these words to him he changed his attitude and became a follower.

The mind is called 'vile' because it is led by ignorance.

389. Here, 'truth and dharma' are synonymous with not lying and being kindhearted. A true Brahmin is called 'clean', because of having a clear mind. External methods of cleaning the external form are not enough.

390. This verse was spoken near Gaya when, during a religious festival, thousands were taking a dip in the holy Gaṅgā to purify past wrong doing. *Com.* has 'If it eliminates past wrongs it will wash off past good too!'

391. The Buddha is the most important of all religious kings and Brahmins.

392. 'Complete the Vedic [path]' means to achieve even the highest state in the formless realm. 'Pure work' is the path to liberation; 'without guile' means release from the desire realm; 'abides' means without mental agitation that comes from any feeling other than equanimity. This teaches release from the realm of form. 'At a (certain) time' means from the ultimate point of view.

393. A Brahmin is popularly known as a person who recites certain words. The *bKa' 'gyur* reads, 'Call him *'Bu'.' 'Bhūr'* is the first syllable of one of the mantras a caste-Brahmin would recite.

394. The 'power of restraint' is 'accumulated'. When one has the four kinds of patience, one is like a king who has amassed his forces. Then all non-virtue is stopped and virtue is done.

395. 'With both'; an example is Anāthapiṇḍada who, while a lay person, served the community of monks. to 'associate' here means to disturb one's detachment.

396. There was a monk who, prior to taking ordination, had been a victorious king. His wife came to where he was staying and carried with her their son. They did not speak. When she put the child on the ground before him, he said, 'We are monks who have no attachment.' Then his wife took the child and left.

397. 'Not keeping others' means that the monk or nun is one with good, pure ordination. 'Abide at the heart' is to abide in

nirvana which is the heart of the practice. 'Fault' is another birth.

398. Many Brahmins were seen crossing over the Sthūlakoṣṭa river. When they returned this verse was spoken. 'Here and there' is the six consciousnesses and their respective objects, and both 'combined', taken as objects of attachment.

399. 'Littlest bit', answers the doubt—'But shouldn't one adhere to virtuous deeds?' Since the results are included in cyclic existence, even virtuous deeds are to be abandoned.

400. 'Virtue and wrongs' are 'both combined' by those persons, like kings who do both great virtue and great non-virtue.

401. Never again will there be a time when afflictive emotions affect the mind of one 'released from bonds'. 'Earlier' means up to the age of forty; 'later' is when life seems nearly gone and one wants to make up for lost time; 'middle' would be any time in between these.

402. Tib: *smyung bu'irtse;* another translation is the 'tip of bamboo'.

403. *sDe dge* edition of the *bKa' 'gyur* has *dad ga* 'faith', instead of *dang ba,* 'clarity'. The moon, considered as a living member of the eastern pantheon, could have the attribute of flawless faith.

404. The holy being was sitting deep in meditation on signlessness when Brahma and three hundred other gods came to his retreat and expressed their pleasure at his work. To be 'seated' is to have detachment of body. To be 'free of dust' is to be free of desire through meditation on uncleanliness; 'think' means the four stages of the path of preparation; 'do work' is the reference to the path of seeing; 'end contamination' is the path of meditation; 'the final body' is the result—the path of no more learning.

405. Tib: *rjes thob,* 'subsequent attainment' here means nirvana.

406. 'Selfless' means that one has achieved the path of seeing.

407. 'Eliminate desires' refers to the desire for many objects that dazzle the lay person. 'Desire's contamination' is the uncontrolled mind 'dripping' to objects. This verse describes the Non-returner (to the realm of desire).

408. A minister of a king in charge of executions was received by Buddha. In order to subdue him Buddha manifested the agony of hells with all the cries of agony and tortures. On seeing and hearing it the minister felt revolted. Then Buddha asked him what was his work; he replied that he was the royal

executioner. Fearful of the consequences of his actions he became a monk.

409. The 'help' given by a true Brahmin is the teaching of the path to liberation.

410. Craving is a 'citadel' because it is hard to overcome.

411. Tib: *chags pa,* 'longing', here means wanting what has not been attained.

412. After taking birth in hell a child was born human and was plagued with recurring fits of high fever. After these were cured by bathing in water, the state of Stream Enterer was attained.

413. *Gandharvas* are ghost-like gods who enjoy great pleasures.

414. 'See' refers to the many types of meditation and equipoise.

415. This verse explains what is entailed by 'all-knowing'.

416. The 'three knowledges' are of three paths or of the three times.

417. The true Brahmin is an 'elephant' because of his or her huge amount of good qualities, a 'great saint' because all the subtle afflictions have been eliminated, and 'untrammelled' because nothing causes animosity to arise.

418. A meditator cultivating the meditative stabilization of what does not come from preparation declined from the signs of attainment and began to disparage the practice. Buddha said, 'Ascertaining some form or some idea means that this meditation is being incorrectly done.' There are three hindrances to meditation: thinking judgmentally, discussing, or deciding to do wrong. 'Meditate' here means to decide to do something after thinking about it.

419. This verse names the four aspects of a Superior's lineage.

420. An ascetic was scourging himself with thorns in the hope of attaining liberation. Buddha taught him the true path with this verse.

421. There is no future migration.

422. See note 304.

423. 'Quite unseen' means hard to understand; 'subtle' is beyond the understanding of sense consciousness; 'the basis' is nirvana; 'realized' is of the cessation of misery; 'awake' means complete wisdom; 'always mindful' means that this one will not degenerate; 'free from clasps' means that all the abandonments of the paths have been obtained.

424. A load is tied to a cart by a rope, net or mesh. The 'mesh' is

made of the pieces of rope in the net part; the 'cords' are the ends of the rope which are tied. Tib: *rgyang thag*, 'drawing'; *Com.* says it means hard to cut or get rid of.

425. See note 244.

426. 'Tiger' is animosity, which eats all the root of virtue.

427. A proud caste-Brahmin became upset with a Foe Destroyer and beat him. Those who harm Brahmins are 'fools' because in the future they will be disparaged, and they are 'bad', because they go to bad migrations.

428. 'Conscious' means that they have heard about and then understood all phenomena.

429. Buddha was living in a shrine to a cannibal spirit (*rākṣasa*) called Bakula who was terrorizing the children of Magadha. After waking from his sleep the Buddha went for a walk. By his deeds he overcame the influence of that spirit and released all from their fears.

430. 'phenomenon' (*dharma, chos*) could also be translated as 're-ligion'; this translation then yields 'perfection in the religious path'.

431. *Com.* refers to another verse here; *zag pa rnams thams cad nub pa nyid du 'gyur*—'and all contamination disappears'. 'Contamination' is said to mean latencies.

432. 'Conditions' refers to the means by which the karma for another birth ripens.

433. 'Clasping' is the result of the condition. Here taking birth is meant.

434. 'Sun' is wisdom free from desire, 'moon' is compassion and 'armour' is patience. The shining of the mind of the true Brahmin is the result-state when birth and death are no more.

435. Buddha was at Rajgir at full moon for the bi-monthly confession ceremony. At night some monks meditated in deep equipoise on the fire element. By their meditation all Rajgir was lit up. The king who was out that night approached that place and listened to these two verses with great faith.

436. The first two lines refer to disinterested compassion which is extended equally to friend and enemy. The last two lines refer to the ending of mental attachments and to the ending of afflictive emotions. They are causes and together with their results they are known as relative truths.

437. Buddha, preparatory to his enlightenment, went and sat for

seven days beneath the bodhi tree meditating on the twelve links from the point of view of their unfolding and their removal (see compilation of verses about nirvana). Early in the morning he arose from the meditation and said these last seven verses.

438. 'This religion' means meditation on the twelve links.

439. This refers to the four truths as seen in the meditation on the twelve links.

440. This teaches the path of seeing which first contemplates true misery, then true origin, etc.

441. The 'conditions' are the contact which give rise to feeling.

442. 'Contamination' means the smallest afflictions eliminated by the path of meditation. 'Doubt' is cast even further away by the path of meditation, therefore it says in this verse also 'freed from every doubt'.

443. *Com.* is slightly different from the *bKa' 'gyur*. It has *blo yang kun bskyed bching las rnam grol ste*.

When a Brahmin with diligence and thought,

Freed from bonds and having all awareness,

Is present [in a state] free from demons

That one has emerged well from all religion.

'Demons' are the thirty-six divisions of the demon hosts.